Adapted From the 1947 Lux Radio Broadcast by

Lance Arthur Smith

Original Lyrics, Music & Arrangements by

Jon Lorenz

www.stagerights.com

MIRACLE ON 34TH STREET

For all stage performance inquiries, please contact:

Steele Spring Stage Rights
3845 Cazador Street
Los Angeles, CA 90065
(323) 739-0413
www.stagerights.com

ORIGINAL PRODUCTION CREDITS AND HISTORY

Miracle on 34th Street: A Live Musical Radio Play was commissioned and first produced by San Diego Musical Theatre at the Horton Grand Theatre, San Diego, CA. It was presented from December 1-23, 2016 and adapted from the 1947 Lux Radio Hour Broadcast by Lance Arthur Smith, with original lyrics, music, and arrangements by Jon Lorenz. The cast was as follows:

Lise Hafso as Olivia Glatt, Eric Hellmers as Wallace Ainsley, Janaya Jones as Cordelia Ragsdale, Matthew Malecki as Grady Williams, Cris O'Bryon as Alex Mialdo, Julia Van Skike as Gracie DeMarco, and Jim Chovick as Kristofer van Lisberg.

The Production was directed by Colleen Kollar Smith, with assistant direction by Brian Rickel, music direction by Jon Lorenz, lighting design by Christina J. Martin, scenic design by Michael McKeon, costume design by Beth Connelly, properties by David Medina, and sound design by Kevin Anthenill. Matthew Bantock was the Stage Manager, Bret Young the Production Manager, Sammy Bauman-Martin the Assistant Stage Manager, T.J. Fucella the Sound Engineer, TNT Scenic the Master Carpenters, and Kate Bower was the Usher Coordinator.

MIRACLE ON 34TH STREET

CHARACTER DESCRIPTIONS

Minimum Casting Requirements: 2F, 2M, 1 Piano/Foley Artist (5 total).
Current Breakdown: 2F, 2M, 1 Older M, 1 Child F, 1 Piano/Foley Artist (7 total).

Character Descriptions and Vocal Ranges
(radio stars named first)

KRISTOFER VAN LISBERG AS KRIS KRINGLE: Santa Claus. Non-singing

CORDELIA RAGSDALE AS DORIS WALKER: Macy's public relations expert. Alto/mezzo-soprano C4-C#5

GRACIE DEMARCO AS SUSAN WALKER: Her precocious daughter (Age 8). C4-C5

GRADY WILLIAMS AS FRED GAILEY: Lawyer, looking for love and a miracle. Baritone/tenor Bb3-G4

WALLACE AINSLEY AS MALE CHARACTER ACTOR: Various. Versatile. Baritone B3-E4

OLIVIA GLATT AS FEMALE CHARACTER ACTOR: Various. Versatile. Soprano C4-E5

ALEX MIALDO AS FOLEY ARTIST: Plays keyboard, foley sounds, and serves as **ANNOUNCER**. Bass/baritone F2-E4

CHARACTER DESCRIPTIONS (CONT'D)

Additional Character Pool, played by the company:

DRUNKEN SANTA: Tight as a knot.
SHELLHAMMER: Macy's PR man.
R.H. MACY: Owner of the department store.
ALFRED: Kris' coworker.
SAWYER: Stuffy head of the personnel department.
MISS PRONG: His secretary.
MOTHER: Thick NY accent. Shopper.
MORTIMER: Her son. Wants toys.
GIRL: Also wants toys.
2ND MOTHER: Girl's mum.
DR. PIERCE: Psychiatrist and friend to Kris.
GIMBEL: Owner of Gimbels, Macy's hated rival.
NURSE: At Bellevue Hospital.
JUDGE: Hard as granite.
CHARLEY: Judge's friend, an Irish priest.
THOMAS MARA: Prosecuting attorney.
MRS. MARA: His wife.
TOMMY: Their son.
POSTMAN: Jovial, knows the denizens of NYC well.
VARIOUS REPORTERS, PHOTOGRAPHERS, CROWD

**NOTE: All actors except the two playing KRIS and SUSAN play multiple roles.*

MIRACLE ON 34TH STREET

SETTING

A radio studio in NYC, circa 1947, then NYC, same.

APPROXIMATE RUN TIME

51 min first act, 44 min second act; 1 hour 35 min total

AUTHOR NOTES

The moment the audience enters the theatre, they've stepped into a magical 1940s radio studio, a studio where stories spring to life through favorite stars of stage and screen. Miracle on 34th Street is a story both familiar and distant– our hope is that in using the conceit of a radio play, a conversation, almost, will begin between actors and audience. A comforting conversation.

In creating the score, our aim was to avoid standard musical theatre sound and try to invoke the authentic musical stylings of the 1930s in a way that connects to audiences in the 21st century. We found the piece is most fun when the actors fully embrace the jazzy vocal stylings of the 1930s: the crooning sound of Bing Crosby, Ella Fitzgerald, Mickey Rooney and Judy Garland; the tightness of the Boswell Sisters and even modern masters like Manhattan Transfer. Authenticity with heart.

MIRACLE ON 34TH STREET

SONG LIST: ACT I

#1. KSDMT "EVENING OF RADIO" THEME & INTRODUCTIONS .... Announcer
#2. TUPPERWARE JINGLE .... Quintet
#3. MACY'S PARADE SONG PT 1 .... Quintet
#3A. "MAGIC" CUE 1 .... Instrumental
#4. MACY'S PARADE SONG PT 2: SANTA! .... Quintet
#5. MACY'S PARADE SONG PT 3: FINALE! .... Quintet
#5A. "MAGIC" CUE 2 .... Instrumental
#6. DINNER WITH DORIS .... Instrumental
#7. TOY DEPT. SONG PTS 1-2 .... Quintet
#8. MUSIC BOX UNDERSCORE (SOUND EFFECT) .... Instrumental
#8A. TOY DEPT. BUMPER .... Instrumental
#8B. MUSIC BOX UNDERSCORE (SOUND EFFECT) .... Instrumental
#9. A LITTLE MAKE BELIEVE .... Fred & Doris
#10. OFFICE BUMPER A (DORIS) .... Instrumental
#11. OFFICE BUMPER B (RH MACY) .... instrumental
#11A. OFFICE BUMPER C .... Instrumental
#12. OUTRO TO FIRST BREAK .... Instrumental
#13. RCA JINGLE .... Quintet
#14. INTRO TO PART 2 .... Instrumental
#15. A CASE OF CHRISTMAS .... Olivia
#16. CANE STORY UNDERSCORE .... Instrumental
#17. OFFICE BUMPER D .... Instrumental
#18. JAZZY KING WENCESLAS .... Olivia & Quartet
#18A. THE IMAGINE NATION .... Instrumental
#19. SLEEPY KING WENCESLAS .... Quintet
#20. FINAL KING WENCESLAS .... Cordelia & Quartet
#21. MACY'S JINGLE .... Quintet
#21A. "MAGIC" CUE 3 .... Instrumental
#22. GIMBELS JINGLE .... Quintet
#23. JINGLE MASH-UP .... Quintet
#24. ALFRED & KRIS .... Instrumental
#25. FINALE: YOU BETTER WATCH OUT! .... Quintet

MIRACLE ON 34TH STREET

SONG LIST: ACT II

#26. KSDMT BUMPER II .... Quintet
#27. T.I.G. JINGLE .... Quintet
#28. REST YE MERRY, GENTS .... Wallace & Quartet
#29. DON'T LET US DOWN .... Fred & Kris
#30. TRANSITION TO ACT II SC 2 .... Instrumental
#31. SNOWFLAKE UNDERSCORE .... Instrumental
#32. HEADLINE NEWS .... Quintet
#33. JAZZY HALLS .... Doris & Announcer
#33A. BREAK UP UNDERSCORE .... Instrumental
#34. MELANCHOLY HALLS .... Doris & Announcer
#35. CAMEL CIGARETTES JINGLE .... Quintet
#36. INTRO TO PT 4 & THE MARA'S .... Instrumental
#37. COURT BUMPER A .... Instrumental
#37A. IN MACY'S HEAD .... Instrumental
#37B. COURT BUMPER B .... Instrumental
#37C. COURT BUMPER C .... Instrumental
#38. MARCH & TANNENBAUM .... Instrumental
#39. I BELIEVE IN YOU .... Susan & Doris
#40. IDEA & ZIPPING .... Instrumental
#40A. REUNION UNDERSCORE .... Instrumental
#41. USPS MARCH .... Quintet
#42. TIDINGS OF COMFORT AND JOY .... Quintet
#43. FAITH UNDERSCORE .... Instrumental
#44. HARK! THE HERALD ANGELS SING .... Quartet
#44A. THE CANE RETURNS .... Instrumental
#45. MIRACLES .... Fred, Doris & Quintet
#46. CAROL-PALOOZA .... Company

SOUND: SPEAKER/MICROPHONE HUM; BEEPS; THE SOUNDS OF A STUDIO RAMPING UP FOR A SHOW

Preshow announcement.

ANNOUNCER: Good evening, ladies and gentlemen! Thanks so much for being part of our live studio audience! How many of you have been with us before here at KSDMT? Wonderful! We thank you for that. For those of you unaccustomed to the rituals of a live radio broadcast, you play an important part. When you see these two signs illuminated like so—

The APPLAUSE SIGNS blaze.

Yes! That's it! Now all of you!

APPLAUSE SIGNS again.

Good, good! Now a quick one!

One more time.

Wonderful! Equally important, if you find something funny, feel free to laugh and laugh loud so Uncle Tim and Aunt Betty, who are listening at home, can hear you. Before we go on air and bring out our stars, I'd like to remind you to please dismantle the sound from any electronic gizmo you may have on your person. I'd also like to point out that this exquisite studio is equipped with emergency exits behind you. *(Noticing the booth)* Oh! And it looks like... yes, here we go! We're on air in five, four, three...

Mouths "two, one."

MUSIC #1: KSDMT "EVENING OF RADIO" THEME & INTRODUCTIONS

Good evening ladies and gentlemen, and welcome to the KSDMT Radio Hour, live from our Horton Grand studio in dazzling downtown San Diego! You'll love tonight's story, that classic Christmas tale of magic and hope—Miracle on 34th Street!

APPLAUSE SIGN blazes.

And now please join me in welcoming our stars— You've heard his crazy characters over your radios for years, and seen his surprising "Boris the Veterinarian" on screen. Wallace Ainsley!

APPLAUSE SIGN.

WALLACE: Call me Wally, folks. My, is it just me or are you hot in here? It's definitely me.

ANNOUNCER: She sings, she dances, she's the comedienne of Canada, that fearless female of funny, Olivia Glatt!

OLIVIA: I'm Olivia Glatt!

APPLAUSE SIGN.

ANNOUNCER: With a list of credits as deep as a Wild West watering hole, the handsome star of Ron Hoard's The Salmon Saloon, Mr. Grady Williams!

GRADY: Good evening, folks.

APPLAUSE SIGN.

ANNOUNCER: Star of stage and screen, she currently treads the Broadway boards in the new smash musical Adagio, Ms. Cordelia Ragsdale!

CORDELIA: Good evening!

APPLAUSE SIGN.

ANNOUNCER: Sometimes called "the other DeMarco sister," you've seen her in MGM's long-running Sissy the Seven-Year-Old Space Pirate series, America's spunkiest space explorer, little Gracie DeMarco!

APPLAUSE SIGN.

Who shines the blinding light of justice into the twisted eyes of evildoers? Beware the glare... of the Bulb!

APPLAUSE SIGN.

Here's the Bulb himself, Mr. Kristofer van Lisberg!

APPLAUSE SIGN.

And you know me, tickling the ivories and electrifying your senses, week after week in the studio I call home, I'm Alex Mialdo!

APPLAUSE SIGN.

And now, KSDMT Radio Hour presents... "Miracle on 34th Street," brought to you by TUPPERWARE!

SONG #2: TUPPERWARE JINGLE

CORDELIA:
IF YOU WANT FRESHNESS WHEN SAVING YOUR MEAL

WOMEN:
GRAB YOUR TUPPERWARE AND USE OUR BURPING SEAL

MEN:
PACK IT IN THERE!

WOMEN:
WHERE?

QUARTET:
TUPPERWARE!
THAT'S WHERE!

ACT I

SCENE 1

EXT. 5TH AVENUE, NYC – DAY

(ANNOUNCER, DORIS, DRUNKEN SANTA & KRIS)

SOUND: PARADE SOUNDS. WALLA—CROWD BUZZING/CHEERING

ANNOUNCER: It's Thanksgiving Day in bustling New York City. On a broad avenue adjoining Central Park, an annual event is joyfully awaited by thousands— the spectacular parade presented by Macy's Department Store to herald in the Christmas season.

SONG #3: MACY'S PARADE SONG - PT 1

MEN:
LOOK OUT THE WINDOW!
JOIN THE BRIGADE

QUINTET:
EVERYONE'S WATCHIN'
THE MACY'S PARADE!

MEN:
IT'S THAT TIME OF THANKSGIVING
WHEN EVERYONE MEETS
HERE IN MANHATTAN
RIGHT OUT IN THE STREETS
TO SPREAD GOODWILL AND CHEER
THE MOST WONDERFUL TIME OF THE YEAR

WOMEN:
WE'VE GOT MARCHING BANDS AND CADETS

MEN:
AND WE'VE EVEN GOT THE ROCKETTES

QUARTET:
AND THEN ALL AROUND YOU FROM OUT OF THE SKIES
YOU WON'T BELIEVE YOUR EYES...

WOMAN 1:
EVERYWHERE

MEN:
EVERYWHERE

WOMAN 1:
UP IN THE AIR

MEN:
IN THE AIR

WOMAN 1:
GIANT BALLOONS THAT ARE BIG AS A HOUSE
HAROLD THE FIREMAN AND MICKEY MOUSE

QUARTET:
CHARLIE THE ELF AND A CATERPILLAR

MEN:
A LUSTY PIRATE

WOMEN:
HE'S QUITE A KILLER
LOOK UP AT THE RIGHT TIME
AND WITH ANY LUCK
YOU'LL SEE A SAILOR BY THE NAME OF,
"DONALD DUCK!"

MAN:
(QUACKS)
LOOK! UP IN THE SKY!

OTHERS:
WHERE? WHERE?

MAN 1:
IT'S A BIRD!

MAN 2:
IT'S A PLANE!

QUARTET:
IT'S SUPERMAN!

TRIO:
AND FELIX THE CAT
THE WONDERFUL, WONDERFUL CAT...

QUARTET:
SO, BEFORE YOU POP THE CORK
IF YOU HAVEN'T SEEN MACY'S,
YOU HAVEN'T SEEN NEW YORK!

ANNOUNCER: Tucked away from the crowd, however, is Doris Walker, of Macy's Public Relations division, who has organized the entire parade. While waiting for her department head, Mr. Shellhammer, she's dealing with a less than joyful situation...

DORIS: You can barely stand! You smell to high heaven of booze, and—

DRUNK SANTA: And nothing! I've been Santa in this parade for—

DORIS: For the last time! You're fired!

DRUNK SANTA *(moving away, exiting)*: Oh, fired, huh? Fine! I didn't need this job anyway! The nerve. Firing a guy because he likes the occasional sidecar. And the occasional martini. And the...

DORIS *(to herself)*: Wonderful. Mr. Shellhammer is on his way and the centerpiece of our celebration is three sheets. Now where am I going to find a white-bearded, jolly Saint Nick?

KRIS *(coming up)*: Pardon me.

MUSIC #3A: "MAGIC" CUE 1

I couldn't help overhearing.

DORIS: You? You... *(Examining him)* are perfect. And what a magnificent cane! Have you... have you any experience as Santa?

KRIS: Oh, I've a bit. Kris Kringle.

DORIS: Doris Walker. A pleasure. Now please, hurry! The parade's about to begin!

SCENE 2

EXT. 5TH AVENUE – LATER

(DORIS & SHELLHAMMER)

SONG #4: MACY'S PARADE SONG – PT 2: SANTA!

MEN:
NOTHING GOES TOGETHER LIKE SANTA AND MACY'S

WOMEN:
NOTHING GOES TOGETHER LIKE SANTA AND MACY'S

MAN 2:
JOY TO THE WORLD, THE TIME HAS COME

QUARTET:
SANTA CLAUS IS COMING

WOMAN:
LOOK IT'S SANTA CLAUS,
HERE COMES SANTA
RIGHT DOWN THE LANE

MAN 1:
LOOK AT THE CRAZY CROWD
I THINK THEY'RE GOIN' INSANE!

QUARTET:
JINGLE BELLS, JINGLE BELLS
JINGLIN' EVERYWHERE

WOMAN:
OH, WHAT FUN IT'S GONNA BE
TO FOLLOW SANTA TO HERALD SQUARE
JINGLE BELLS, JINGLE BELLS
JINGLIN' EVERYWHERE

DUET:
EVERYBODY'S GOING SO I HOPE WE SEE YOU THERE!
EVERYBODY'S GOING SO I HOPE WE SEE YOU THERE!

DORIS: What do you think, Mr. Shellhammer?

SHELLHAMMER: He's simply wonderful, Mrs. Walker! Just look at him on that float! The most realistic Santa Claus we've ever had. Why, he didn't even need any padding, did he?

DORIS: Padding?

SHELLHAMMER: Why, didn't you notice his tummy? So round, so jolly! It shakes when he laughs!

DORIS: Like a bowl full of jelly?

SHELLHAMMER: Just like. Where on earth did you find him?

DORIS: I— I don't know. He tapped me on the shoulder with that beautiful cane, I turned around, and there he was.

SHELLHAMMER: And to think our old Santa showed up to work tight!

DORIS: Tight as a knot.

SHELLHAMMER: Just imagine if Mr. Macy had seen him!

DORIS: Just imagine if Mr. Gimbel had seen him! Competition between our two stores is tough enough!

SOUND: BIG BAND

SHELLHAMMER *(laughing)*: Well, the parade's starting. Let's stand at the curb.

DORIS: Not I, Mr. Shellhammer.

SHELLHAMMER: But you worked so hard on the parade!

DORIS: Yes, and that's why I'm going home to relax. Besides, I can see it from there. I live right around the corner.

SHELLHAMMER: Ah yes! Of course! Happy Thanksgiving, Mrs. Walker. I'll see you tomorrow. And congratulations on finding the best Santa in Macy's history!

SONG #5: MACY'S PARADE SONG – PT 3: FINALE!

WOMAN 2:
NOTHING GOES TOGETHER LIKE SANTA AND MACY'S

MAN 2:
MORE THAN BUTTER AND BREAD

WOMAN 1:
MORE THAN HEPBURN AND TRACY

QUARTET:
SO, BEFORE YOU POP THE CORK
IF YOU HAVEN'T SEEN MACY'S,
YOU HAVEN'T SEEN NEW YORK!

SCENE 3

FRED GAILEY'S APARTMENT, PARK AVENUE – SAME (FRED, SUSAN & DORIS)

ANNOUNCER: The parade continues past the window of one Fred Gailey, whose Park Avenue apartment is just down the hall from Doris Walker's...

FRED: It certainly is a lovely parade, Susan. Look at that baseball player balloon.

SUSAN: It was a clown balloon last year. Mother said they repainted it to look like Joe Dimaggio so they could capitalize on the Yankees' World Series win.

FRED *(beat)*: Well baseball player or clown, it's certainly a giant!

SUSAN: Giant, Mr. Gailey? There are no such things as giants.

FRED: Well, not now, maybe, but in olden days there were—

SUSAN: Oh come now, Mr. Gailey. And you, a lawyer!

FRED: Well, what about the giant that Jack killed? In the fairy tale?

SUSAN: First off, Jack was a thief, a boy who broke in to someone's home and took things that didn't belong to him. Secondly, I agree with my mother— it's just a fairy tale and fairy tales are silly nonsense.

FRED: Well, that baseball player sure looks like a giant to me.

SOUND: DOORBELL BUZZ

(Calling out)

Come in! It's open!

SOUND: DOOR OPENING.DOOR CLOSES.HEELS WALKING

DORIS: Hello. I'm Doris Walker, Susan's mother. My housekeeper said—

SUSAN: Oh hello, mother! I'm watching the parade. Mr. Gailey invited me.

DORIS: Hello darling.

FRED: Susie's told me quite a lot about you, Mrs. Walker.

DORIS: She's told me quite a lot about you too— the man in the front apartment.

SUSAN: The parade's much better than last year.

FRED: May I get you some coffee?

DORIS: Please, if it isn't too much trouble.

FRED: No trouble— it's already made.

SOUND: COFFEE CUPS CLINKING. COFFEE POURING

FRED: Here you are.

DORIS: Thank you. *(Drinking)* I also want to thank you for being so kind to Susan. I'm not around as often as I'd like, and she doesn't play with a lot of children.

FRED: Well, in truth, this was part of a plot. Susie and I have become great friends since I moved in last year, but I– I've wanted to meet you for some time, Mrs. Walker.

DORIS: Hm. At least you're Frank.

FRED *(quickly)*: Fred.

DORIS: a courtesy chuckle.

SUSAN *(calling out)*: There goes another one of your silly giants, Mr. Gailey!

FRED: Susan tells me you don't approve of fairy tales.

DORIS: I don't. I think we should be realistic and completely truthful with our children.

MUSIC #5A: "MAGIC" CUE 2

SUSAN: There goes Santa Claus!

DORIS: Oh, don't even mention that name in front of me!

SUSAN: Why not, Mother?

DORIS: Well, that Santa Claus you see is a last-minute substitution.

SUSAN: But why?

DORIS: Well... you remember how the janitor was last New Year's?

SUSAN: Oh my! Tight as a knot! But look at this one. He fits the part. *(Quickly)* If that's your sort of thing.

DORIS: That's right. She never has.

SOUND: END OF PARADE

SUSAN: Well, that's the end of the parade. *(Beat)* Mother?

DORIS: Yes?

SUSAN: I've been thinking. It's Thanksgiving and there are only two of us. Couldn't we invite Mr. Gailey?

DORIS: Well, I–

FRED: Oh, uh, please don't bother. I'll– I'll just slap together a sandwich or something.

SUSAN: Mother, we have such a big turkey. Please, mother, it'd be a waste.

DORIS: Well, I– I–

SUSAN *(whispering)*: Did I ask her all right, Mr. Gailey? I decided to add the bit about the size of the turkey to strengthen the appeal.

FRED: Susie! That part was confidential.

DORIS *(amused)*: You asked fine, Susan. Dinner's at three, Mr. Gailey. We'll expect you there not a minute later.

SUSAN: Or earlier!

MUSIC #6: DINNER WITH DORIS

SCENE 4

DORIS' APARTMENT, PARK AVENUE – LATER

(DORIS, SUSAN, FRED & SHELLHAMMER ON PHONE)

ANNOUNCER: Later, at dinner down the hall in Doris' apartment...

SUSAN: I don't know, Mr. Gailey. What did one vegetable say to the other on their long walk?

FRED *(mouth full)*: Lettuce rest, I'm feeling beet.

All three laugh.

SUSAN: Very punny, Mr. Gailey.

FRED: Well played, Susie! *(To Doris)* Mrs. Walker, this meal beats the pants off the sandwich I would've made.

DORIS: Well, thank you! This was a wonderful idea you had... Susan.

SUSAN laughs.

I really am having a wonderful—

SOUND: PHONE RINGS/RECEIVER PICKUP

Oh excuse me, won't you?

FRED: Of course! So Susie, tell me...

FRED & SUSAN continue, WALLA-WALLA in bg.

SHELLHAMMER *(filter)*: Mrs. Walker?

DORIS: Yes, Mr. Shellhammer?

SHELLHAMMER *(filter)*: Your maid told me you were having Thanksgiving dinner, and I apologize for interrupting, but I just had to tell you. Your Santa Claus was stupendous!

DORIS: Thank you.

SHELLHAMMER *(filter)*: Mr. Macy himself wants him to be our toy department Santa Claus!

DORIS: Oh, fine! Can you hire him?

SHELLHAMMER *(filter; laughs)*: Oh, I already have! The way he captivated the crowd today... oh, he's a born salesman, I can feel it!

DORIS: Good. We'll talk about it in the morning. Thanks for calling, Mr. Shellhammer.

SONG #7: TOY DEPT. SONG – PT 1

MEN:

SANTA'S IN HIS WORKSHOP
WORKING WITH HIS ELVES

WOMEN:

MAKING SURE THE TOYS THEY MAKE

QUARTET:

WILL GET UP UPON THE SHELVES

MEN:

TOYS MADE FOR ALL CHILDREN
BY THE ELVES THAT HE EMPLOYS
WHO SEND THEM ALL TO MACY'S
THE HOME OF CHRISTMAS JOYS

SCENE 5

MACY'S DEPARTMENT STORE – DAY AFTER THANKSGIVING

(ALFRED, SHELLHAMMER & KRIS)

ANNOUNCER: It's the day after Thanksgiving at Macy's Department Store, a day beloved by employees and customers alike, and Kris prepares for his first day of work...

ALFRED: Here he is, Mr. Shellhammer. Here's Santy Claus.

SHELLHAMMER: Thank you, Elfred. Ah, Alfred! *(To Kris)* He's Alfred the Elf. Well, good morning *(Sugary)* Santa Claus.

KRIS: Good morning, Mr. Shellhammer!

SHELLHAMMER: Now, before you make your way to the toy department, here is a list of toys that we have to push.

SOUND: PAPER UNROLLING/CRINKLING

KRIS: Push?

SHELLHAMMER: You know, these are things we're overstocked on. Now, you'll find that a great many children will be undecided as to what they want for Christmas. When that happens, you immediately suggest one of the items on the list. Do you understand?

KRIS *(with disapproval)*: Oh, I certainly do.

SHELLHAMMER: Fine, that's fine. Now take the list and Elfred–

ALFRED: Alfred!

SHELLHAMMER: Alfred here will show you to your throne in the toy department. *(Walking away)* And don't forget– you're working at Macy's now!

KRIS: Imagine that– making a child take something she doesn't want, all in the name of profit! That's what I've been fighting against for years.

ALFRED: What's that, Mr. Kringle?

KRIS: The commercialization of Christmas!

SONG #7: TOY DEPT. SONG - PT 2

MEN:

TOYS, TOYS, TOYS!
FOR ALL THE GIRLS AND BOYS

QUARTET:

LET YOUR SHOPPING TRIP COMMENCE
BRING YOUR DOLLARS AND GOOD SENSE

MEN:

FOR TOYS, TOYS, TOYS!
FOR ALL THE GIRLS AND BOYS

WOMEN:

'CAUSE THE HOLIDAYS ARE PERFECT
TO DO WHAT MAKES LIFE WORTH LIVING

QUINTET:

SO, COME ON DOWN TO MACY'S
IT'S THE SEASON FOR GIVING!

MUSIC/SOUND #8: MUSIC BOX UNDERSCORE

SCENE 6

MACY'S TOY DEPARTMENT – LATER

(MORTIMER, MORTIMER'S MOTHER, KRIS, SHELLHAMMER, ALFRED & GIRL)

MORTIMER: Are you really Santa Claus?

KRIS: Why of course I am! Now, what would you like for Christmas, little boy?

MORTIMER: I want a red fire engine with a fire hose that squirts real, live water! And I won't do it in the house, honest. Only in the backyard. I promise!

KRIS *(laughing)*: I can tell you're a very good boy. So I promise you'll get your fire engine!

MORTIMER: You see, Mama! I told you he'd get me one!

MOTHER *(thick NY accent)*: That's fine. That's just dandy. You wait over there, Mortimer. Mama wants to thank Santa for his "help" personally.

KRIS: Yes, madame? Did you also want to make a Christmas request?

MOTHER: Look, my kid wants a fire engine but there isn't one to be had anywhere in town. Macy's ain't got one. Gimbels ain't got one. Ain't nobody got one! My feet are killin' me, and you say "Okay, the kid gets one"? Can't you sell him something you have here?

KRIS: But my dear, you can get those fire engines at Schnitkopf's, Lexington Avenue. Only four-fifty apiece. A real bargain!

MOTHER: Schnitkopf's?

KRIS: Yes indeed!

MOTHER: Hey. I— I don't get it.

KRIS: Oh, I follow the toy market quite closely.

MOTHER: No, I mean, Macy's is sending people to other stores? Are you kiddin'?

KRIS: Well, the important thing is for the child to be happy. Whether Macy's or someone else sells the toy doesn't matter, does it? As long as the child gets the toy. Don't you think that way?

MOTHER: Who, me?

KRIS: Yes, you!

MOTHER: Oh yeah, sure, but I didn't know Macy's did. *(Moving away)* I don't get it. I just don't get it. Mortimer! Put down that rocket!

SHELLHAMMER: Come on Elfred, keep the children moving along. Who's next, please?

ALFRED: Yes, Mr. Shellhammer. Come along, little girl, it's your turn to see Santa Claus.

KRIS: Hello, little girl! And what would you like?

GIRL: Rollerskates!

KRIS: Then you shall have them!

GIRL *(moving away)*: Mama! Mama! Santa's gonna bring me some roller skates!

2ND MOTHER: That's wonderful! *(Confidentially to Kris)* And you have some fine skates here at Macy's, don't you Santa Claus?

KRIS: Oh, they're good skates, all right, but— but not quite good enough. Now, I left some really wonderful skates at Gimbels. I'm sure Gimbels will have just what this wonderful little girl desires. Merry Christmas!

SHELLHAMMER *(to himself)*: Gimbels? That's what you said, isn't it? Gimbels.

MOTHER: Mr. Shellhammer? Excuse me, are you Mr. Shellhammer?

SHELLHAMMER *(in disbelief)*: Gimbels? That's what he did say. Gimbels.

MOTHER: The saleslady said I should speak to you.

MORTIMER: Mother!

SHELLHAMMER *(louder, to himself)*: Gimbels.

MOTHER: Hold your horses, Mortimer. Mr. Shellhammer, I just wanted to congratulate you and Macy's on this wonderful new stunt you're pulling!

SHELLHAMMER *(to Mother)*: Gimbels.

MOTHER: Imagine, a big outfit like Macy's putting the spirit of Christmas ahead of the commercial.

SHELLHAMMER: Gimbels?

MOTHER: From now on I'm gonna be a regular Macy's customer.

MORTIMER: Mother!

MOTHER *(moving away)*: All right, Mortimer, we're going.

SHELLHAMMER *(to the heavens)*: Gimbels!

MUSIC: Music Box Fades Into...

MUSIC #8A: TOY DEPT. BUMPER

MUSIC/SOUND #8A: MUSIC BOX UNDERSCORE

ANNOUNCER: Later that day...

SUSAN: And here's the toy department, Mr. Gailey.

FRED: You certainly know all about Macy's, Susan.

SUSAN: As you know, my mother works here and I'm very observant. But I still think it's silly that you'd bring me here to meet Santa Claus, when you could easily drop me off in my mother's office upstairs.

FRED: Well, I just feel that when you've talked with him, you might start to believe.

SUSAN: I doubt that. But I'm a reasonable person, Mr. Gailey, and I'm certainly willing to try.

SOUND: ELEVATORS, CROWD NOISE, LOUDER AS WE MOVE TO SANTA'S AREA

ALFRED: Come along, little girl, it's your turn!

KRIS: Well, well! What a charming young lady, eh? And what's your name, little girl?

SUSAN: Susan Walker. What's yours?

KRIS: Mine? Kris Kringle. I'm Santa Claus.

SUSAN *(skeptically)*: Uh-huh.

KRIS: Oh ho! You don't believe that, eh?

SUSAN: Uh-uh. My mother's Doris Walker, you see. The lady who hired you.

KRIS *(amused)*: Oh, oh, oh.

SUSAN: But I must say, you're the best looking Santa I've ever seen. The most believable, at any rate.

KRIS: Really?

SUSAN: Well, your beard for instance. It doesn't have one of those strings that goes over your ears.

KRIS *(laughing)*: That's because it's real! Just like I'm really Santa Claus. Go ahead— give it a pull. *(She does)* Ouch!

SUSAN: Oh my— oh my goodness! It is real!

KRIS *(laughing)*: Yes, yes! Now please let go!

SUSAN: Oh! I apologize!

KRIS *(chuckling)*: That's quite all right. Now what would you like me to bring you for Christmas?

SUSAN: Nothing, thank you. Whatever I want, my mother will get— as long as it's sensible and doesn't cost too much.

KRIS: Oh.

DORIS *(entering)*: That's quite right, Susan.

SUSAN: Oh! Hello, mother!

DORIS *(icy)*: Hello, Mr. Gailey.

FRED *(embarrassed)*: Hello. Uh, the explanation for this is very simple. Your housekeeper's mother sprained her ankle. She had to go home, so she asked me to bring Susan down here to you. As long as we were here, I— I figured we might as well say hello to Santa Claus.

SUSAN: He's a nice old man, Mother. He has real whiskers!

DORIS: Yes, dear, a lot of old men have whiskers like that. Susan, would you mind standing over there a minute? I'd like to talk to Mr. Gailey.

SUSAN *(moves off, cheerily)*: Of course, Mother. I'll be over by the dolls. *(Beat)* The sensibly priced ones.

FRED: I, uh, I shouldn't have brought Susie to see Santa, is that it?

DORIS: Now you're making me feel completely heartless.

FRED: I'm sorry.

SONG #9: A LITTLE MAKE BELIEVE

DORIS: Don't you see? I tell Susan that Santa Claus is a myth— and you show her a very convincing old man with real whiskers. Whom is she to believe?

FRED:

I UNDERSTAND AND I APOLOGIZE
I ACTED OUT OF TURN
THIS, I REALIZE

PERHAPS, IT WASN'T MY PLACE
BUT, IF YOU'VE GOT A MOMENT,
I'D LIKE TO PLEAD MY CASE:

DORIS: Proceed, Counselor.

FRED:

THE WORLD IS SOMETIMES ROUGH
AT TIMES IT CAN BE TOUGH
SOME FUN CAN BRIGHTEN UP YOUR FACE
AND HELP IN THE DIFFUSING
OF FEELING LIKE YOU'RE LOSING
A NEVERENDING RACE

THERE'S NOTHING LIKE THE SHORT REPRIEVE
THAT YOU CAN GET FROM
A LITTLE MAKE BELIEVE

DORIS: Mr. Gailey, when Susan was a baby, her father and I were divorced.

FRED: Yes, she told me.

DORIS: And ever since then I've protected my child by teaching her realities.

FRED: Even when reality is banality?

DORIS:

WE DON'T BELIEVE IN
FAIRY TALES OR FABLES
'CAUSE FANTASY ENABLES
IDEALS YOU CANNOT OBTAIN

DORIS (CONT'D):

AND I WON'T ADD TO HER CONFUSION
SET HER UP FOR DISILLUSION
AND UNNECESSARY PAIN
IF SHE KEPT WAITING FOR PRINCE CHARMING
TO COME AND SWEET TALK HER...

FRED:

WEREN'T WE TALKING ABOUT SUSIE, MRS. WALKER?

DORIS: Yes. Well...

FRED:

SO YOU DON'T BELIEVE IN FLYING REINDEER?

DORIS:

NO, WE'RE BOTH SANE HERE

FRED:

NOT DONNER OR CUPID?

DORIS:

MR. GAILEY, DON'T BE STUPID.

FRED:

NOT DANCER OR PRANCER?

DORIS:

I THINK YOU KNOW THE ANSWER.

FRED:

NOT EVEN A BIT?

DORIS: I'm her mother.

(Singing)

I'LL RAISE HER AS I SEE FIT.

FRED: Of course.

DORIS: Thank you.

FRED:

BUT WHY NOT ENTERTAIN SOME...

DORIS:

I'D PREFER TO ABSTAIN FROM...

BOTH:

A LITTLE MAKE BELIEVE

FRED:

IT'S NOT A CRIME TO HAVE...

DORIS:

WE DON'T HAVE TIME TO HAVE...

BOTH:

A LITTLE MAKE BELIEVE

DORIS: I must ask you to respect my wishes.

FRED: Of course. I meant no offense.

DORIS: Good evening, Mr. Gailey. *(Moves off, to Susan)* All right, dear, the store's going to close soon; we'll run along to my office.

SUSAN: Yes mother. Goodbye, Mr. Gailey!

MUSIC #10: OFFICE BUMPER A (DORIS)

SCENE 7

DORIS WALKER'S OFFICE, LATER

(DORIS, KRIS & SUSAN)

ANNOUNCER: Toward the conclusion of the busy day, Kris makes his way up to Doris Walker's office...

SOUND: TYPEWRITERS

SOUND: KNOCK ON DOOR. DOOR OPENS

KRIS: Alfred said you wanted to see me, Mrs. Walker.

DORIS: Oh, um, oh, yes. Come in.

SOUND: OFFICE DOOR SHUTS. TYPEWRITERS OUT

KRIS: You have a delightful little girl, Mrs. Walker.

DORIS: Thank you. Susan's the reason I asked you to see me. I'd be grateful if you'll please tell her that you're not really Santa Claus— that there actually is no such person?

KRIS *(amused)*: Oh, but, Mrs. Walker, not only is there such a person, but here I am to prove it!

DORIS: No, you misunderstand. I want you to tell her the truth. Now, what's your real name?

KRIS: Kris Kringle. And I always tell the truth. Susan, I'll bet you're in the first grade.

SUSAN: Second grade!

DORIS: I mean your real name.

KRIS: Well, that is my real name. My goodness, the second grade?

DORIS *(losing patience)*: Very well. I have your employment card right here. I'll look it up on that.

KRIS: That's a very pretty dress you have on, Susan.

SUSAN: It's from Macy's. We get ten percent off.

KRIS: Oh.

SUSAN: I like your cane, Mr. Kringle. I don't know that I've ever seen one so fancy.

KRIS: Do you want to know a secret? I carved it from—

DORIS: Susan, would you go out and talk with Mrs. Harney for a moment?

SUSAN: Of course. She always gives me a treat and... oh no. That part was confidential.

DORIS: That's all right, dear. You may have one.

SOUND: DOOR OPENS. TYPEWRITERS

KRIS: Good-bye, young lady! I hope to see you again soon!

SUSAN: I hope so too! Goodbye.

SOUND: DOOR SHUTS. TYPEWRITERS OUT

DORIS: So! You always tell the truth, do you?

KRIS: Mm hm.

DORIS: Look at your employment card.

KRIS *(reading)*: "Name: Kris Kringle. Address: Brooks Memorial Home, Great Neck, Long Island." You may call the home and ask for Dr. Pierce if you'd care to confirm that, Mrs. Walker. It's a home for elderly gentlemen.

DORIS: Would you also like me to confirm this?

KRIS: What's that?

DORIS *(reads, with disdain)*: "Date of Birth: As old as my tongue and a little bit older than my teeth."

KRIS *(chuckling)*: Yes.

DORIS *(reads)*: "Place of Birth: North Pole." Now, really.

KRIS: Why, I believe you doubt me, Mrs. Walker.

DORIS: And this tops everything. *(Reads)* "Next of Kin: ..."

KRIS: Oh, that.

DORIS *(read)*: "Dasher, Dancer, Prancer and Vixen."

KRIS: And Comet, Cupid, Donner, and Blitzen, but the line wasn't long enough.

DORIS: ...I'm sorry to have to do this, Mister—

KRIS: Kringle.

DORIS: But, I'm afraid we'll have to let you go.

KRIS: Have I done something wrong?

DORIS: No, no, it's just that we feel—

SOUND: PHONE RINGS

(Exhales)

Oh, excuse me.

SOUND: RECEIVER UP

Hello?

SHELLHAMMER *(filter)*: This is Mr. Shellhammer, Mrs. Walker! Drop whatever you're doing! Mr. Macy wants to see you immediately!

DORIS: Oh, I'll be right up.

SOUND: RECEIVER CLICKS DOWN

DORIS (CONT'D) *(back to Kris)*: I'm afraid I'll have to be very abrupt with you; I have to see Mr. Macy. You'll be paid for the full week, Mr. Kringle, and I'll send your check to that address on your employment card.

KRIS: Oh...

MUSIC #11: OFFICER BUMPER B (R.H. MACY)

SCENE 8

R.H. MACY'S OFFICE – LATER

(MACY, DORIS & SHELLHAMMER)

ANNOUNCER: When R.H. Macy calls you up to his office, you hop to it, and that's precisely what Doris does, as she heads to the top floor.

SOUND: ELEVATOR DING. HIGH HEELS WALKING. DOOR KNOCK

MACY: Oh, uh, come right in, Mrs. Walker.

SOUND: DOOR OPEN

DORIS: Thank you, Mr. Macy.

SOUND: DOOR CLOSE

MACY: Now, about this new policy you have initiated.

DORIS: Er, oh–

MACY: Macy's Santa Claus sending customers to Gimbels–

DORIS: I can explain everything, Mr. Macy.

MACY: You don't have to explain a thing. Just look at my desk. Forty-two telegrams and over five hundred phone calls. Grateful parents expressing undying gratitude to Macy's department store.

DORIS: Why, you don't say?

MACY: And from now on, not only will our Santa Claus continue in this manner but every salesperson in the entire store.

DORIS: You mean that if we haven't got what the customer asks for, we're to–?

MACY: We're to send him where he can get it. No high pressuring and forcing a customer to take something he doesn't really want.

DORIS: I think that's wonderful, Mr. Macy.

MACY: Why, we'll be known as, as the helpful store! The friendly store! The store that places public service ahead of profits! *(In a moment of discovery)* And, consequently, we'll make more profits than ever. Heh! *(Back to business)* As for you and Mr. Shellhammer, you'll find a more practical expression of my gratitude in your Christmas envelopes.

DORIS: Oh! Thank you.

MACY: And tell that wonderful Santa Claus I won't forget him, either. Matter of fact, I'll tell him myself in the morning.

DORIS *(quietly)*: Oh...

MACY: Goodnight, goodnight!

SOUND: DOOR OPEN

DORIS *(weakly, moving out)*: Goodnight, Mr. Macy. And thank you again, sir.

SOUND: DOOR SHUTS

SCENE 9

INT. DORIS' OFFICE – MINUTES LATER

(SHELLHAMMER & DORIS)

MUSIC #11A: OFFICE BUMPER C

ANNOUNCER: Doris finds Mr. Shellhammer back in the Public Relations department and relates the good news first...

SHELLHAMMER: Oh! Imagine, a bonus!

DORIS *(weakly)*: Yes...

SHELLHAMMER: Well, what's the matter with you?

DORIS: I just fired him.

SHELLHAMMER: Who?

DORIS: Santa Claus.

SHELLHAMMER *(raging)*: Oh, no, no, no, no. No, you couldn't have!

DORIS: But I did! He— he's crazy, Mr. Shellhammer. He's a sweet old man, but he really thinks he is Santa Claus.

SHELLHAMMER: I don't care if he thinks he's Maureen O' Hara! You've got to get him back.

DORIS: It's too great a risk. Don't you understand, Mr. Shellhammer? He's out of his mind. What if he should have a— a fit or something? Oh, no. I've got to tell Mr. Macy.

SHELLHAMMER: Don't do that! Maybe this Mr. Kringle is only... only a little crazy. Anyway, you can't be sure until he's examined. We'll send him to Mr. Sawyer in personnel.

DORIS: Sawyer?

SHELLHAMMER: He's paid to examine employees, isn't he?

DORIS: Well yes, but—

SHELLHAMMER: Good. *(Beat)* Well don't just stand there, find him! Find him! Or Mr. Macy is going to present us with a very unmerry Christmas!

MUSIC #12: OUTRO TO FIRST BREAK

ANNOUNCER: Has Doris Walker gone down in history as simultaneously the best and worst thing to ever happen at Macy's? Will she be able to track down Kris Kringle in time? Find out when "Miracle on 34th Street" continues after this commercial break.

APPLAUSE SIGN blazes.

And now, a word from our sponsors.

Commercial break.

SONG #13: RCA JINGLE

OLIVIA: Come in, R.C.A. calling.

MEN:
HEY, U.S. OF A
YOU'VE GOT A CALL FROM THE FUTURE

WOMEN:
CALL FROM THE FUTURE

MEN:
WHEN COMMUNICATIONS ARE WOUNDED
WE'LL BE THE SUTURE

WOMEN:
WE'LL BE THE SUTURE

FRED:
WHEN YOU'RE TACTICAL
WE'RE PRACTICAL
ON AIR OR SEA OR LAND
YOU WANT SECURE TRANSMISSIONS?

WOMEN:
WE'VE GOT THE VISION
WE'LL KEEP YOU IN POSITION

QUARTET:
TO COMPLETE THE MISSION TASK AT HAND
PERFORMANCE YOU REQUIRE AND VALUE YOU EXPECT
WHILE THE WORLD KEEPS SPINNING AWAY
THANKS TO RCA!

ANNOUNCER: RCA— for all your tactical military communications and surveillance needs.

QUARTET *(whispers)*:
RCA!

ANNOUNCER: And now, Part Two of "Miracle on 34th Street"!

MUSIC #14: INTRO TO PART 2

After dismissing the best Santa Claus in Macy's history, Doris Walker contacted Dr. Pierce at the Brooks Memorial Home and now rushes to meet Mr. Kris Kringle. Under the beautiful trees outside the home...

SCENE 10

EXT. BROOKS MEMORIAL HOME – DAY

(KRIS & DORIS)

DORIS: Thank you for seeing me, Mr. Kringle. I'm afraid I acted rather hastily, and perhaps unfairly. Well Mr. Macy and I would like you to stay on.

KRIS *(considering)*: Hm. This is… this is mighty good news!

DORIS: Oh thank goodness!

KRIS: You see, Mrs. Walker, for fifty years or so I've been more and more worried about Christmas. Christmas is not just a thing, it's a frame of mind. And that's what they've been changing. Well I'm glad you're taking me back— maybe I can do something about it. And I'm glad I met you and your daughter. You're my test case!

DORIS: We are?

KRIS: Yes! In a way, you're the whole thing in miniature. And if I win you over— well, there's still hope! *(Sadly)* If not, then I guess I'm through. But I'll try! And I warn you— I don't give up easily!

DORIS *(laughing, in spite of herself)*: I do admire your passion! Now first thing tomorrow, please report to Mr. Sawyer in Personnel for an exam.

KRIS: Mental examination?

DORIS: Well partly, yes.

KRIS: Oh I don't mind. I've taken dozens. Haven't failed one yet. And I won't fail this one!

SONG #15: A CASE OF CHRISTMAS

OLIVIA:

HELP ME DOCTOR,
I'M COMIN' DOWN WITH SOMETHIN'
THAT'S MESSIN' WITH MY BUSINESS
I CAN'T STOP BEIN' KIND
THINK I'M LOSIN' MY MIND
I THINK I'M COMIN' DOWN
WITH A LITTLE CASE OF CHRISTMAS

SCENE 11

SAWYER'S OFFICE – MORNING

(KRIS, SAWYER & MISS PRONG)

ANNOUNCER: Dusting off his sharpest suit, Kris finds his way to the Personnel Department and to Mr. Sawyer's office...

KRIS: So you see, Mr. Sawyer, I dusted off my sharpest suit and came right up here to see you!

SAWYER *(insecure, and incredibly disagreeable)*: Oh. Well, then, that's your own beard, huh?

KRIS: Hm? Oh, yes, yes.

SAWYER: Mm. Interesting complex in back of that. Why do you carry a cane?

KRIS: Always carry a cane, Mr. Sawyer. Well, that is, when I wear street clothes.

SAWYER: Hmph.

MUSIC #16: CANE STORY UNDERSCORE

KRIS: I carved this cane out of a runner from one of my old sleighs.

SAWYER: What's that? What's that?

KRIS: With a fine, solid silver top.

SAWYER: Hm. Who was the first president of the United States?

KRIS: What? Oh, give me a difficult one. Like who was— who was vice president under James Monroe?

SAWYER: It was... uh, I... *(Catching himself)* I'm conducting this examination!

KRIS: The answer is Daniel D. Tompkins.

SAWYER *(sputters, grumbles)*: Well, I— I—!

KRIS: Yes. You're a— You're a rather nervous man, aren't you, Mr. Sawyer?

SAWYER: Hm?!

KRIS: Tell me, do you, um— do you get enough sleep?

SAWYER: My personal habits are no concern of yours! Now, what hand am I holding up?

KRIS: Right hand.

SAWYER: How many fingers do you see?

KRIS: Three. Oh dear, oh dear. You bite your nails, too...

SAWYER *(more sputters and grumbles)*: Well, I—! *(Quickly)* Stand up, now. Feet together. Arms extended.

KRIS: Muscular coordination test. I've taken dozens of these tests. You know very often nervous habits like yours are caused by insecurity. *(Beat, then)* Mr. Sawyer— are you happy at home?

SAWYER: What?! That will be all, Mr. Kringle! The examination is over!

SOUND: DOOR OPEN

KRIS: Thank you.

SAWYER: And before you leave, it may interest you to know I've been happily married for twenty-two years! Very happily married!

KRIS *(exiting)*: Delighted to hear it. Goodbye, Mr. Sawyer!

SOUND: DOOR CLOSE. INTERCOM BUZZ

SAWYER *(yells)*: Miss Prong!

MISS PRONG: Yes sir?

SAWYER: Get Mrs. Walker on the phone!

MISS PRONG: Yes, sir. But your wife, Mr. Sawyer, she's called four times already.

SAWYER: Well, you tell my horrible wife to leave me alone and mind her own business!

MISS PRONG: Here's Mrs. Walker, sir.

SAWYER: Oh. All right. *(Clears throat)* Hello.

DORIS *(filter)*: Oh, I was just going to call you, Mr. Sawyer.

SAWYER: Oh?

DORIS *(filter)*: There's a Dr. Pierce stopping by my office this afternoon at three.

SAWYER: Who's Dr. Pierce?

DORIS *(filter)*: She's the physician at the Brooks Home. I thought we might discuss Mr. Kringle's case with her.

SAWYER: Well, there's hardly any point in discussing it, Mrs. Walker. Obviously, the old man should be discharged!

MUSIC #17: OFFICE BUMPER D

SCENE 12

DORIS' OFFICE - AFTERNOON

(DORIS, PIERCE & SAWYER)

ANNOUNCER: Discharged!? Thankfully Dr. Pierce stops by Doris' office to set the record straight.

DORIS: How long have you known him, Dr. Pierce?

PIERCE: Well, he wandered into the home about, oh, I suppose it was eight months ago. Looked the place over and said "Hm, this'll do." Just stayed on.

DORIS: Has he ever told you his real name?

PIERCE: He said he was Kris Kringle. We never pressed him further.

SAWYER: Dr. Pierce, as I told Mrs. Walker, Kringle should be dismissed immediately and sent to a mental institution.

PIERCE: Oh, now just a minute, Mr. Sawyer. People are institutionalized to keep them from hurting themselves or others.

SAWYER *(dismissive)*: He's deluded. Saying that he's Santa Claus!

PIERCE: It's a delusion for good. I found he only wants to be friendly and helpful.

SAWYER: His whole manner suggests aggressiveness. Look at the way he carries that cane. Mrs. Walker, naturally, I can't discharge that loony, so when he exhibits his maniacal tendencies, and I assure you he will, please realize the responsibility is completely yours!

SOUND: DOOR SLAMS SHUT

DORIS: Well, I'm right back where I started.

PIERCE: Mrs. Walker, I assure you, Kris Kringle has no maniacal tendencies.

DORIS: But if there's the slightest possibility of his causing any trouble—

PIERCE: What trouble?

DORIS: All that need happen is a policeman asks his name. "Kris Kringle"— clang clang! —and Macy's Santa Claus lands up in the psychopathic ward.

PIERCE: Well, you can prevent that very simply. Now, there must be someone here at the store who could rent him a room. Then they could both come to work together. I'd just as soon he avoided that long train ride to Long Island, anyway.

DORIS: You mean, sort of, take custody of him?

PIERCE: Mm hm.

DORIS: Do you think that Mr. Kringle would agree to that?

PIERCE: Oh, I'm sure he'll agree.

DORIS: Well, in that case— Now, let me see. Who do I know who could rent him a room?

SONG #18: JAZZY KING WENCESLAS

OLIVIA:

GOOD KING WENCESLAS LOOKED OUT
ON THE FEAST OF STEPHEN
STEPHEN!
WHEN THE SNOW LAY ROUND ABOUT
DEEP AND CRISP AND EVEN

QUARTET:

BRIGHTLY SHONE THE MOON THAT NIGHT!

OLIVIA:

THOUGH THE FROST WAS CRUEL

MEN:

THE FROST WAS CRUEL!

QUARTET:

WHEN A POOR MAN CAME IN SIGHT

OLIVIA:

GATHERING WINTER FUEL

SCENE 13

THE WALKER HOME – DINNER; LIVING ROOM AND KITCHEN (CONTINUOUS)

(KRIS, DORIS, SUSAN & FRED)

MUSIC #18A: THE IMAGNE NATION

SUSAN: I'm glad you're going to have dinner with us, Mr. Kringle.

KRIS: Oh, thank you, Susan.

SUSAN: I'm also very glad you're going to live next door with Mr. Gailey.

KRIS: Oh? Why?

SUSAN: Because you're nice to talk to.

KRIS: Oh. *(Chuckles)* I say, what a fine young man that Mr. Gailey is, eh? Just think, allowing me to share his apartment— a mere stranger.

SUSAN *(quietly)*: He did it because Mother hinted to him.

KRIS: Ohhh. Well, anyway, I'm very grateful. What do you think of Mr. Gailey?

SUSAN: He's become a dear friend of mine. Better than most of the children at school, actually.

KRIS: Oh.

SUSAN: Shall I tell you what I did in school today?

KRIS: Oh, by all means. Any games?

SUSAN: Yes. And a very silly game, too.

KRIS: Oh?

SUSAN: They played "Zoo." And each child was supposed to be an animal!

KRIS: Oh, but, Susan, they were just pretending.

SUSAN: But that's what makes the game so silly.

KRIS: Oh. Well, of course, in order to play games, you need imagination.

SUSAN: Oh, uh, that's when you see things but they're not really there, huh?

KRIS: Well— yes. Yes, but, you know, to me, imagination is a place all by itself. Now, you've heard of the French nation?

SUSAN: Mm hm.

KRIS: And the British nation?

SUSAN: Yes.

KRIS: Well, this— is the Imagination! ...A very interesting place, too.

Music out.

Now, how would you like to be able to make snowballs in summertime, eh?

SUSAN: What?

KRIS: Or be the Statue of Liberty in the morning— and, in the afternoon, fly south with a flock of geese?

SUSAN: Well, I'm quite sure I'd like it, but—

KRIS: Oh, it's very simple. Really. Well, anyway, look here, the next time they play "Zoo," you can be a monkey.

SUSAN: But I don't know how to be a monkey!

KRIS: Don't you? Oh, I'll show you. Now first, you bend over a little like, uh, like this, see? Now, let your arms hang loose, see?

SUSAN: Like this?

KRIS: Yeah, that's fine. Fine. Now, put your hand over here— and start scratching, see? That's it. That's it! That's excellent, Susan. That's as fine a bit of scratching as I've ever seen. Now— now, you start chattering.

SUSAN: Chattering?

KRIS: Yes. Now, listen.

Chatters like a monkey.

See? And keep scratching. Now then, look here, we'll do it together, see? Chatter and scratch. And scratch and chatter. See?

He continues chattering. SUSAN starts chattering.

(Laughing)

That's fine, Susan, fine, you're doing beautifully! Beautifully! Yes!

KRIS and SUSAN continue chattering and laughing in bg.

DORIS: Goodness me, they're making a racket in there.

FRED: Sounds to me like they're having quite a bit of fun. Are you sure you don't want any help cooking?

DORIS: No thank you. I'm just about done. But you can help set the table.

SOUND: SILVERWARE CLANKING

Before the monkeys arrived, you were telling me about your position.

FRED: My...? Oh, yes! The firm of Haislip, Haislip, Sherman and Mackenzie has been very good to me. But being an exceptional lawyer, I naturally want to open my own office!

DORIS: Naturally. *(Calling out)* All right, chimpanzees, swing over to the table— it's dinner time!

ALL BUT DORIS laughter and chattering.

SUSAN: Try it, Mother! Just try it.

DORIS: Oh no, Susan, I don't—

FRED: Like this?

Chatters loudly.

DORIS chattering. Builds to bigger chattering.

ALL join in laughing and chattering.

SONG #19: SLEEPY KING WENCESLAS

WOMEN:
BRIGHTLY SHONE THE MOON THAT NIGHT

MEN:
BRIGHTLY SHONE THE MOON THAT NIGHT

WOMEN:
BRIGHTLY SHONE THE MOON THAT NIGHT

MEN:
BRIGHTLY SHONE THE MOON THAT NIGHT

ALL:
BRIGHTLY SHONE THE MOON

Music fades into dialogue.

SCENE 14

THE WALKER HOME, SUSAN'S BEDROOM – BEDTIME

(KRIS, DORIS, SUSAN & FRED)

KRIS *(quietly)*: Susan? Susan? Are you still awake?

SUSAN *(sleepily)*: Uh huh.

KRIS: I just wanted to say good night, Susan, before Mr. Gailey and I take our leave. Now look here, about Christmas. There must be something you'd like for Christmas. Something that even your mother doesn't know about. Why don't you give me a chance.

SUSAN: Well, I've certainly thought about something, Mr. Kringle.

KRIS: You have? Well, what is it, eh? Tell me.

SUSAN: It's right here on the night table, see?

KRIS: Oh?

SUSAN: I tore this page out of a magazine. It's a picture of a house.

KRIS: Oh ho! That's what you want, is it? A doll's house. Colonial architecture.

SUSAN: Oh, not a doll's house. A real house.

KRIS: A real house?

SUSAN: Yes. And if you're really Santa Claus, you can get it for me.

KRIS: Now, now, now, wait a minute, Susie. What could you possibly do with a big house?

SUSAN: Live in it with my mother. And a backyard with a big tree to put a swing on, and a garden, and a... *(Defeated)* Oh, well. Why even discuss it?

KRIS: Susie— Susie, could I, uh, could I keep this picture? Just, uh— Just in case?

SUSAN: I guess so.

KRIS: Thank you, dear, thank you. Well, Mr. Gailey's waiting for me. Goodnight, Monkey!

Chatters like a monkey.

SUSAN *(amused)*: Goodnight, Mr. Kringle! Eep eep!

SONG #20: FINAL WENCESLAS

CORDELIA:

THEREFORE, GENTLEMEN, BE SURE
WEALTH OR RANK POSSESSING
YOU, WHO NOW WILL BLESS THE POOR
SHALL YOURSELVES FIND BLESSING.

WOMEN:

YOU, WHO NOW WILL BLESS THE POOR

TRIO:

SHALL YOURSELVES FIND BLESSING.

SCENE 15

FRED'S APARTMENT – EVENING

(KRIS & FRED)

FRED: Take whichever bed you want, Mr. Kringle.

KRIS: You're very kind, really. Tell me, Mr. Gailey, just what is it you do for a living?

FRED: Oh, I'm a lawyer. Haislip, Haislip, Sherman and Mackenzie.

KRIS: Oh. Oh. And you, uh, you like living here in the city?

FRED: Well, it's convenient. But someday I'd like to get a place on Long Island.

KRIS: Huh!

FRED: Not a big house. Just one of those junior partner deals around Manhasset.

KRIS: Oh, one of those little colonial houses, hey?

FRED: Yeah, yeah. A little colonial house would be swell.

KRIS: Good, good, yes. You're, um— You're quite fond of Mrs. Walker, aren't you?

FRED *(chuckles)*: A lot of good it does me. She lives in a cast iron shell that's just a little difficult to penetrate.

KRIS: Oh. Well, if you care for her then you must try harder, Mr. Gailey. Like a lot of divorced people, Mrs. Walker is determined not to be hurt again. You know, she and that child are a couple of lost souls. And it's up to us to help them.

FRED: Oh?

KRIS: I'll take care of Susie if you take care of her mother. And in turn, both of them shall take care of you.

FRED: Me? Do I need taking care of?

KRIS: Of course! You're lost too, Fred.

FRED: In what way?

KRIS: We all need someone to believe in us. You. Them. Me. *(Through a smile)* Now, shall I turn out the light?

FRED: No, no, no.

KRIS: No?

FRED: I'm not gonna be cheated out of this. You know, all my life I've wondered about it, and now I'm going to find out. Tell me, does Santa Claus sleep with his whiskers outside or inside the covers?

KRIS: Ohhh. Outside, of course. Outside, by all means. The cold air makes them grow.

SCENE 16

MR. MACY'S OFFICE – MORNING

(MACY & DORIS)

ANNOUNCER: Early morning, back on the top floor of Macy's Department Store...

SONG #21: MACY'S JINGLE

OLIVIA:

IT'S SMART TO BE THRIFTY
IT'S SMART TO BE SURE
IF YOU'RE SICK OF SHOPPING
WE'LL BE THE CURE

GRADY:

TEN BEAUTIFUL FLOORS
THE WIDEST SELECTION
OF QUALITY GOODS

CORDELIA:

THE SERVICE?

WALLACE:

PERFECTION!

MEN:

IF WE'RE OUT OF STOCK
DON'T BEGIN TO SORROW

WOMEN:

WHEN WILL MACY'S HAVE IT?

MEN:

DAY AFTER TOMORROW!

WOMEN:

IF YOU WANT TO

ALL:

"PAY CASH, PAY LESS."
THERE'S ONLY ONE WAY, SEE

WOMEN:

IT'S SMART TO BE THRIFTY

MEN:

IT'S SMART TO BE SURE

ALL:

IT'S SMART TO SHOP MACY'S

MACY: Oh, come in, Mrs. Walker, come in.

DORIS: Thank you, Mr. Macy. I've just heard something very exciting.

MACY: You have? Well, let me tell you something very exciting. Our policy of being kind to customers has tripled our sales! Now, what do you think of that?

DORIS: That's wonderful, Mr. Macy. And Gimbels thinks it's wonderful, too.

MACY *(uneasy)*: Gimbels?

DORIS: Gimbels is adopting the same policy.

MACY: Well, is that so?

DORIS: And it gives me an idea. As long as Gimbels is doing the same thing, why not some pictures for the newspapers?

MACY: Pictures?

DORIS: Yes! You and Mr. Gimbel— shaking hands.

MACY *(disbelief)*: Shaking hands?! R. H. Macy and— and Gimbel?

DORIS: Well— Well, yes.

MUSIC #21A: "MAGIC" CUE 3

MACY: Yes, yes, why not? With Santy Claus! It's a great idea, Mrs. Walker! *(Not entirely sold)* Macy and Gimbel— shaking hands!

SONG #22: GIMBELS JINGLE

MEN:

THERE'S NO ONE ELSE THAT UNDERSELLS GIMBELS!
THE DEPARTMENT STORE THAT EXCELS: GIMBELS!
COME ON DOWN TO 33RD, FACING GREELY SQUARE
EVERYTHING THAT YOU MIGHT NEED,
GIMBELS HAS IT THERE!
NOT JUST A STORE, AN INNOVATOR: GIMBELS!
THE FIRST TO HAVE AN ESCALATOR: GIMBELS!
ELEVEN FLOORS THE STAFF IS BRIGHT AND NIMBLE
"SELECT, DON'T SETTLE" AT GIMBELS! GIMBELS!

SCENE 17

EXT. MACY'S DEPARTMENT STORE, 34TH ST, NYC – MORNING

(MACY, GIMBEL, KRIS, PHOTOGRAPHERS, REPORTERS & CROWD)

WALLA-WALLA: buzz of photographers ("Thank you, Mr. Gimbel." "Stand right there." "Smile.").

MACY: Oh, that's enough pictures, gentlemen. Thank you. Thank you very much.

WALLA-WALLA: Photographers move off and fade out.

Well, Mr. Gimbel?

GIMBEL: Come on, R. H. Now we'll go over to my store and get some really good pictures.

MACY: Oh, heh. Just a minute. I have something here for Santy Claus. Here you are, Mr. Kringle. A check in appreciation of all you've done.

KRIS: Mr. Macy! Why, that's most kind of you.

GIMBEL: I didn't think you were that generous, R. H. That's quite a check. What are you gonna do with it, Mr. Kringle?

KRIS: Well, I have a friend. A Dr. Pierce. She needs a new x-ray machine.

MACY: Buy the machine through the store. Ten percent discount.

GIMBEL: Nonsense. Come over to Gimbels. We'll furnish it at cost.

KRIS *(jovially)*: Oh, keep it up, gentlemen, keep it up. ...At this rate, my friend'll have a whole new hospital!

ALL laugh.

SONG #23: JINGLE MASHUP

WOMEN:

IT'S SMART TO BE THRIFTY

IT'S SMART TO BE SURE

IT'S SMART TO SHOP–

MEN:

GIMBELS! GIMBELS!

COME ON DOWN TO 33RD

WOMEN:

COME TO HERALD SQUARE

TEN BEAUTIFUL FLOORS, THE WIDEST SELECTION

MEN:

ELEVEN FLOORS THE STAFF IS BRIGHT AND–

WOMEN:
IT'S SMART TO SHOP—

MEN:
SELECT, DON'T SETTLE AT GIMBELS

WOMEN:
MACY'S

MEN:
GIMBELS

WOMEN:
MACY'S

MEN:
GIMBELS

WOMEN:
MACY'S

ALL:
GIMBELS/MACY'S

MEN:
GIMBELS

SCENE 18

MACY'S DEPARTMENT STORE, EMPLOYEE AREA – LUNCH (ALFRED & KRIS)

MUSIC #24: ALFRED & KRIS

ANNOUNCER: Back in the employee area at Macy's, Kris and Alfred ponder how the publicity photos turned out.

Music out.

ALFRED: How did the publicity photos turn out, Mr. Kringle?

KRIS: Oh, fine, Alfred, fine. How about a game of checkers during lunch, eh?

ALFRED: Oh, not today, Kris. I— I don't feel so good.

KRIS: Oh? What's the matter, Alfred?

ALFRED: Oh, nothin' much. You remember I was telling you how I like to play Santa Claus over at the Y and give out presents to the kids?

KRIS: Yes?

ALFRED: Well, I was tellin' Mr. Sawyer about it and he says that's very bad. That psychologically it's all wrong.

KRIS: Wrong? To be nice to children?

ALFRED: Well, he says guys who play Santa Claus do it because when they was young they must've done somethin' bad and now they do something they think is good to make up for it, see? ...It's what he calls a "guilt complex."

KRIS *(cautiously)*: Alfred— what else has he found wrong with you?

ALFRED: Oh, nothin' much. Just that I hate my father. *(Beat)* I didn't know it, but he says I do.

KRIS: Excuse me.

ALFRED: Hey, ain't you gonna have lunch?

KRIS: Later. Right now, I have an appointment— with Mr. Sawyer!

SONG #25: FINALE: YOU BETTER WATCH OUT!

OLIVIA:
YOU BETTER WATCH OUT,

GRADY:
YOU BETTER NOT LIE

CORDELIA:
YOU BETTER NOT SHOUT, I'M TELLIN' YOU WHY

QUARTET:
SANTA CLAUS IS COMIN'!

CORDELIA:
IF YOU'RE ON HIS LIST

MEN:
WHAT?

GRADY:
THEN YOU'RE OUT OF LUCK!

OTHERS:
OH MY!

GRADY:
YOUR TIME HAS RUN OUT.
YOUR GOOSE HAS BEEN PLUCKED!

OTHERS:
OW!

QUARTET:
SANTA CLAUS IS COMIN'
YOU BETTER WATCH OUT!

SCENE 19

SAWYER'S OFFICE, PERSONNEL – MINUTES LATER
(SAWYER & KRIS)

SOUND: BURSTING THROUGH THE DOOR

SAWYER: What do you mean, breaking into my office like this?

KRIS: Mr. Sawyer, are you a licensed psychiatrist?

SAWYER: What business is it of yours? Now leave, you lunatic, before I have you—

KRIS: I have great respect for psychiatry. And great contempt for meddling amateurs who go around practicing it.

SAWYER: Shut up.

KRIS: You ought to be horsewhipped. Taking a boy like Alfred and filling him up with complexes and phobias—

SAWYER: I think I'm better equipped to judge that than you.

KRIS: Just because Alfred wants to be kind to children, you tell him he has a guilt complex!

SAWYER *(smug)*: Having the same delusion, you couldn't possibly understand.

KRIS: Ohhhhh—

SAWYER: And don't you wave that cane at me!

KRIS: Either you stop analyzing Alfred or I'll go straight to Mr. Macy and tell him what a contemptible fraud you are!

SAWYER: Oh, get out of here, get out of here before I have you thrown out!

KRIS: There's only one way to handle a man like you. Maybe this'll knock some sense into you!

SOUND: THWACK! KRIS' CANE CLOCKS SAWYER'S NOGGIN

SAWYER *(squealing)*: Oooh! Oh, help! Oh, my head, my head. Oh, ho ho!

KRIS *(fading out)*: I take my leave, and I've made my point. Good day, Mr. Sawyer.

SOUND: DOOR CLOSE, ABRUPTLY

WOMEN:

CHRISTMAS IS COMING
AND HE'S HERE TO PROTECT IT
HAS HE SAVED IT, OR

MEN:

HAS HE WRECKED IT?
SANTA CLAUS IS COMIN'

SOUND: BUZZ

SAWYER: Miss Prong, get me the police! Get me Mrs. Walker! Get me the psychopathic ward in Bellevue Hospital! Kris Kringle just signed his own admission slip!

Maniacal laughter.

Music full up.

ALL:

HE POPPED THE DOC
WHO WAS SHRINKIN' HIS NOGGIN!
WILL HE ESCAPE ON HIS MAGIC TOBOGGAN?

ANNOUNCER: Santa Claus committed? Sawyer the pseudo-psychiatrist triumphant? And what of Kris' friends, little Susan, Doris, and Fred? And what about Ms. Prong? Find out when we return to "Miracle on 34th Street" after a brief intermission!

ALL:

HE'S COMIN' TO TOWN!
SO DON'T MESS AROUND!
SANTA CLAUS IS COMIN'

WALLACE:

HE'S COMIN' TO TOWN

ALL:

SANTA CLAUS IS COMIN'

WALLACE:

SO DON'T MESS AROUND

ALL:

SANTA CLAUS IS COMIN' TO TOWN!

END ACT I

VOICEOVER: We're back on air in five, four, three, two, one, and—

APPLAUSE SIGN blazes.

MUSIC #26: KSDMT BUMPER II

ALL: K-S-D-M-T !

SONG #27: T.I.G. JINGLE

ANNOUNCER: And now, a word from our sponsor: T.I.G. Technology Integration Group!

MEN:

LEADERS IN SOLUTIONS AND TECHNOLOGY

WOMEN:
T.I.G., T.I.G.

MEN:
INTEGRATING ALL YOUR TECHNOLOGY

WOMEN:
T.I.G., T.I.G.

MEN:
WE WORK IN THE CREATION
OF SYSTEM INTEGRATION
POWER YOUR ORGANIZATION
FULL OPTIMIZATION

OLIVIA:
FOUNDED BACK IN EIGHTY-ONE

WOMEN:
T.I.G., T.I.G.

OLIVIA:
SO MANY YEARS AND WE'VE JUST BEGUN

MEN:
GOT A NETWORK? WE'LL SECURE IT!

WOMEN:
HARD AND SOFTWARE? WE'LL PROCURE IT!

ALL:
TECHNOLOGY INTEGRATION GROUP ARE WE:
T.I.G!

ACT II

SCENE 1

BELLEVUE HOSPITAL, HOLDING ROOM

(NURSE, FRED & KRIS)

ANNOUNCER: And now, Part Three of "Miracle on 34th Street"!

SONG #28: REST YE MERRY, GENTS

WALLACE:

GOD REST YE MERRY GENTLEMEN
LET NOTHING YOU DISMAY
REMEMBER HOW THE SAVIOR
WAS BORN ON CHRISTMAS DAY
TO SAVE US ALL WHEN WE HAD GONE ASTRAY
SO WITH TRUE LOVE AND BROTHERHOOD
EACH OTHER NOW EMBRACE

MEN:

O, TIDINGS OF JOY
TIDINGS OF JOY
TIDINGS OF COMFORT AND JOY

O, TIDINGS OF JOY
TIDINGS OF JOY
TIDINGS OF COMFORT AND JOY

ANNNOUNCER: Kris Kringle, who has opened the hearts of New York residents, sits alone in a holding room at Bellevue Hospital. However, a visitor has arrived, heralding hope–

NURSE: You can see Mr. Kringle now, Mr. Gailey.

FRED: Thank you, nurse.

SOUND: DOOR OPENS

FRED: Hello, Kris.

KRIS *(sighing)*: Hello, Fred.

FRED: Kris, I've been speaking to the doctors. They said they've given you some tests.

KRIS: Oh, yes. Same old tests.

FRED: Except this time you failed to pass them. Kris, you deliberately failed. Why?

KRIS: Why? Well— because I had great hopes, Fred. I had a feeling Mrs. Walker was beginning to believe in me, and now— Well, now I discover she was only humoring me all the time.

FRED: But this wasn't Doris' idea at all. Mr. Sawyer had you sent up here before she even knew about it. And now there's nothing she can do.

KRIS: Oh. Well, it's not just Mrs. Walker. It's— Well, now, take Mr. Sawyer. He's contemptible, dishonest, deceitful— Yet he's out there and I'm in here. Well, if that's normal— I don't want it.

FRED: But you can't just think of yourself, Kris.

SONG #29: DON'T LET US DOWN

(Singing)

IF THERE'S ONE THING WE CAN COUNT ON
IT'S SANTA CLAUS ON CHRISTMAS DAY
SANTA, IN HIS MAGIC SLEIGH
SANTA, IN HIS SPECIAL WAY
MAKING SPIRITS BRIGHT
EVERY CHRISTMAS EVE NIGHT

KRIS: Fred, what are you doing?

FRED: It's Christmas. I'm singing.

(Singing)

I KNOW YOU'RE TEMPTED HERE RIGHT NOW
TO THINK JUST OF YOURSELF
YOU SPEND YOUR WHOLE LIFE GIVING
TO EVERY BOY AND GIRL
AND ELF

BELIEVE ME, I WOULD UNDERSTAND
IF YOU CALLED IT A DAY

BUT BEFORE YOU THROW IT IN
I'VE JUST GOT TO SAY

DON'T LET US DOWN
DON'T LET US DOWN

DON'T LET THE DOUBT OF SIMPLE PEOPLE TURN YOU 'ROUND
FOLKS LIKE ME BELIEVE IN WHAT YOU STAND FOR

FRED (CONT'D):

IN FACT, ALL NEW YORK THINKS
YOU'RE A GUY TO STRIKE UP THE BAND FOR
SO BRING BACK THOSE ROSY CHEEKS
AND WIPE AWAY YOUR FROWN
DEAR KRIS KRINGLE, DON'T LET US DOWN

SOME FOLKS THINK THAT FAITH IS BEST CONTAINED UNDER A STEEPLE
BUT WHAT HAPPENS TO YOU MATTERS TO MANY PEOPLE
OH, TO BELIEVE IN SOMETHING CAN CHANGE SOMEONE
KIDS LIKE SUSIE, WHO HAVE JUST BEGUN

KRIS: Well, Fred, maybe you're right. I— of course you're right. I ought to be ashamed of myself. Let's get out of here.

FRED: Now, wait a minute, you flunked your mental examination, but good.

KRIS *(with a laugh)*: Oh yes, so I did.

Music stops.

I said our first President was Captain America. Oh but you're a lawyer, you can think of something.

FRED: Hey, look, I can't just—

KRIS:

DON'T LET ME DOWN
DON'T LET ME DOWN,

FRED:

I WON'T LET YOU DOWN
I WON'T LET DOUBT

KRIS:

I WON'T LET DOUBT

BOTH:

TURN ME AROUND

FRED:

THE GREATEST PART OF BELIEVING THE IMPOSSIBLE
IT SERVES AS A REMINDER THAT THERE'S NO ROAD UNCROSSABLE
YOU'RE A HOPE THAT KEEPS US GOING
WHEN WE'RE BREAKING DOWN
DEAR KRIS KRINGLE,

KRIS:

DEAR MISTER GAILEY,

FRED:

DON'T

KRIS:
DON'T

FRED:
I WON'T

BOTH:
LET YOU DOWN

KRIS:
I WON'T LET YOU DOWN

MUSIC #30: TRANSITION TO ACT II SC 2

SCENE 2

FRED'S APARTMENT – JUST AFTER DINNER

(SUSAN, FRED & DORIS)

ANNOUNCER: As had become their custom, Susan, Doris, and Fred clean up after dinner in his apartment.

DORIS: Another delicious meal.

FRED: Thank you. Reheating leftovers is my specialty.

SUSAN: What are you going to do about Mr. Kringle, Fred?

FRED: I'm not quite sure, Susie. *(Moving away)* Perhaps some hot chocolate will thaw my frozen brain. I'll get us all some.

DORIS: Thank you, Fred. Susan, will you hand me that plate, please? *(Beat)* Susan?

SUSAN: Fred is trying his best, isn't he Mother?

DORIS: Of course, Susan. He'll help Kris.

SUSAN: I do hope so. I think Fred can get do great things if he applies himself.

DORIS: I feel the same way. I'll finish cleaning up.

SUSAN: I remember looking down at him from this window during the parade. He was so happy and kind to everyone in the crowd. He doesn't deserve to be treated like this.

DORIS: I agree darling. Now close that window— you'll catch a chill.

MUSIC #31: SNOWFLAKE UNDERSCORE

SUSAN: But it's just started snowing, Mother. Look. *(Beat)* I like to pretend I can see an entire world inside each snowflake.

DORIS: You like to... pretend?

SUSAN: Well, yes. I do now, since Mr. Kringle came along. And it's funny, mother.

DORIS: What's funny, dear?

SUSAN: The children at school seem... different to me now. I look at them like I look at that snowflake— each one is different, each one shows me something new.

FRED *(returning, sipping hot chocolate)*: I've started to look at the world that way as well. That's had more to do with you, Doris.

DORIS: Thank you, though I think Kris has contributed quite a bit. *(Sipping hot chocolate)* This hot chocolate recipe, for instance. It's perfect. *(Chuckling)* It's because he's Santa Claus, of course.

SUSAN *(eagerly)*: Do you really think so, mother?

DORIS: Well, I—

FRED *(drinks, then slowly)*: It's because he's Santa Claus... of course!

DORIS: Fred?

FRED: You know something? You've just given me the idea I've been searching for!

SCENE 3

STREETS OF NYC – MORNING

SONG #32: HEADLINE NEWS

SOUND: RUSTLE OF NEWSPAPERS

QUARTET:
EXTRA, EXTRA!

NEWSBOY #1: Coal in Santa's Stocking,
Bats in his Belfry!

QUARTET:
EXTRA, EXTRA!

NEWSBOY #2: 34 Years for 34th Street Santa?

QUARTET:
EXTRA, EXTRA!
LOOK AT THE NEWS!
SANTA'S IN TROUBLE
AND HE'S BEING RECUSED!
TIME'S RUNNING OUT!
CHRISTMAS IS NEARING!

NEWSBOY #3: "Daily Bulletin! Macy Santa Claus to Have a Lunacy Hearing!"

QUARTET:
EXTRA, EXTRA!
READ ALL ABOUT IT!
THE HEADLINES JUST GET CRAZIER
EACH TIME THAT WE SHOUT IT
CHRISTMAS IS BECOMING
A COMICAL CAPER
READ ALL ABOUT IT
FOR A NICKEL A PAPER

NEWSBOY #3:
EXTRA!

NEWSBOY #1:
EXTRA!

MEN:
SANTA'S GETTIN' HEADLINES
HE'S MANAGED TO DRIVE

WOMEN:
THE UNITED NATIONS STORY
BACK TO PAGE FIVE!

NEWSBOY #3: New York Express!

QUARTET:

"KRIS KRINGLE CRAZY?
COURT CASE COMING!
KIDDIES CRY CALAMITY!"
THE CITY IS HUMMING

NEWSBOY #4: "Evening Dispatch! Doctors Doubt Sanity of Santa Who Launched Goodwill Campaign!"

ALL:

CHRISTMAS IS COMING
THE GOOSE IS GETTING FATTENED
AND SANTA CLAUS IS MAKING
QUITE A STIR IN MANHATTAN
WE'RE DECKIN' HALLS WITH HOLIDAY VALANCE
WHILE SANTA'S FATE IS HANGING IN THE BALANCE

IT MAY PERPLEX YA
IT MAY VEX YA
MERRY CHRISTMAS
EXTRA! EXTRA!

SCENE 4

NEW YORK COUNTY COURTHOUSE

(MARA, JUDGE, FRED, KRIS & GALLERY)

KRINGLE: Good morning, your honor!

JUDGE: Er, good morning. You may proceed, Mr. Assistant District Attorney.

MARA: My name's Thomas Mara. What's yours?

KRIS: Kris Kringle.

MARA: Oh. *(Clearing his throat)* Now then, uh, where do you live, please?

KRIS: Well, it seems to me that's what this hearing will decide, won't it?

Courtroom laughter.

MARA: Mr. Kringle— do you really believe that you are Santa Claus?

KRIS: Of course I do.

MARA: That's all, your Honor, the State rests its case.

JUDGE: In view of this statement, do you still wish to put in a defense Mr. Gailey?

FRED: I do, your Honor. I'm fully aware of my client's opinions. In fact, that is the entire case against him. But Mr. Kringle is not sane because he believes he is Santa Claus.

JUDGE: An entirely logical conclusion.

FRED: Not necessarily, your Honor. You believe yourself to be Judge Harper. Yet no one questions your sanity because you are Judge Harper.

JUDGE: Mr. Kringle is the subject of this sanity hearing, not I.

FRED: Exactly. So I intend to prove that Mr. Kringle is Santa Claus.

Courtroom reactions.

ALL: ("Preposterous!" "Can he do that?" "He does look like Santy.")

SOUND: JUDGE BANGS GAVEL

JUDGE *(quietly)*: Mr. Mara, I thought you said this was a cut and dried sanity hearing.

MARA *(quietly)*: Well, I thought it was, your Honor.

JUDGE *(clears throat, addressing the courtroom)*: In view of Mr. Gailey's statement, I'll have to review the entire background of this case. Court's adjourned till tomorrow morning.

SCENE 5

DORIS' APARTMENT – EVENING.

(FRED & DORIS)

ANNOUNCER: That evening, champagne at the ready, Fred heads to Doris' apartment.

SONG #33: JAZZY HALLS

DORIS:

DECK THE HALLS WITH BOUGHS OF HOLLY
FA LA LA LA LA LA LA LA LA
'TIS THE SEASON TO BE JOLLY
FA LA LA LA LA LA LA LA LA
DON WE NOW OUR GAY APPAREL
FA LA LA LA LA LA LA
TROLL THE ANCIENT YULE TIDE CAROL
FA LA LA LA LA LA LA LA LA

FRED: Hello, darling. I'm sorry I'm late but get ready, we're really gonna celebrate tonight.

DORIS: What are we celebrating?

FRED: Well, didn't you read the papers? "Santa's Mouthpiece Throws Bombshell in New York Supreme Court!"

DORIS: Oh, darling, you're not really serious about this. You can't possibly prove that Kris Kringle is Santa Claus.

FRED: Well, you saw Mr. Macy and Mr. Gimbel shake hands. That wasn't possible either.

DORIS: What does your firm have to say about it— Haislip and Mackenzie, and the rest of them?

FRED: That I've, er, jeopardized their prestige, and either I drop this impossible case or they'll drop me.

DORIS: You see?

FRED: So I beat 'em to it. I quit.

DORIS: Fred! You threw away a career because of a sentimental whim?

FRED: Well, I'll open my own office.

DORIS: And what kind of clients will you get?

FRED: Oh— probably a lot of people like Kris who are being pushed around. Doris, look, don't you have any faith in me at all?

DORIS: Oh, it's not a question of faith. It's— it's just common sense.

FRED: But faith is believing in things when common sense tells you not to. It's not just Kris that's on trial. It's everything he stands for. Human kindness, and love, and dignity—

DORIS: Oh, darling, listen. We've hardly been apart since Thanksgiving. I— Well, I've become incredibly fond of you. We've talked about some wonderful plans for the future, haven't we? And then you do this— go on an idealistic binge, throw away your security, and expect me to be happy about it?

MUSIC #33A: BREAKUP UNDERSCORE

FRED: And I expect too much. Is that it? Why don't you try a little blind faith, darling? I think I have a right to ask that.

DORIS: I think I have the right to ask you to be a little bit more practical and realistic.

FRED *(considering)*: Yes. Yes, I suppose you have. *(Beat)* It's all cock-eyed. Here we are as close as two people could be and yet we're miles apart.

DORIS: There's a loneliness about us, I know. I've tried my best.

FRED: Oh, I know you have. So have I. But we're gonna need a lot more than each other's arms. I don't know if we've got it.

DORIS *(beat)*: Funny. With all my common sense, I was just beginning to think this time it might work out.

FRED: Your head was telling you that?

DORIS: My heart.

FRED *(almost a plea)*: Darling? *(Beat, no answer)* Well, that's that, I guess.

DORIS: I guess it is. Goodnight, Fred.

FRED: Goodnight, Doris.

SOUND: DOOR SOFTLY SHUTS

SONG #34: MELANCHOLY HALLS

DORIS:
FAST AWAY THE OLD YEAR PASSES
FA LA LA LA LA LA LA LA LA
HAIL THE NEW, YE LADS AND LASSES
FA LA LA LA LA LA LA LA LA
SING WE JOYOUS ALL TOGETHER
FA LA LA LA LA LA LA
HEEDLESS OF THE WIND AND WEATHER
FA LA LA LA LA LA LA LA LA

ANNOUNCER: Heads and hearts out of synch? What began as a celebration of victory derailed into a train of heartache. Can this engine find the track? "Miracle on 34th Street" will continue in a moment.

Music up full, finish to commercial break.

APPLAUSE SIGN blazes.

Commercial break.

SONG #35: CAMEL CIGARETTES JINGLE

ANNOUNCER: And now another word from another sponsor: Camel Cigarettes!

WOMAN 1:
WHEN IT COMES TO TOBACCO

MEN:
OO, AH

WOMAN 1:
WHEN IT COMES TO ELATION

MEN:
OO, AH

WOMEN:
TRY THE ONE CIGARETTE
WITH NO BURNING SENSATION

MEN:
SENSATION
A CIGARETTE NAMED FOR A MOISTURE RETAINING MAMMAL

WOMEN:
MAMMAL! MAMMAL!

WOMAN 1:
GIVE YOUR THROAT A VACATION AND SWITCH TO CAMELS

ANNOUNCER *(whispers)*: Camels!

WOMEN:
INHALE WITH EASE
EVEN SANTA AGREES

ANNOUNCER: And now, Part Four of "Miracle on 34th Street"!

MUSIC #36: INTRO TO PART 4 & THE MARA'S

Despite their affection for one another, Doris and Fred can't seem to find a way to reconcile their differing views on faith and practicality. While at his home, Assistant District Attorney Thomas Mara receives what to him is even more unsettling news...

SCENE 6

THE MARA HOME – EVENING

(MARA & MRS. MARA)

SOUND: PHONE RINGS, RECEIVER UP

MARA: Hello? ...Yes, this is Mr. Mara. ...Well, can't it wait till tomorrow? I'm eating din— ...Who's been subpoenaed...? *(Raging)* Well, how do you think I feel about it? I'll see you tomorrow!

SOUND: RECEIVER SLAMS DOWN

MRS. MARA: Who was that, dear?

MARA: R. H. Macy's been subpoenaed!

MRS. MARA: Oh my!

MARA: Those reporters! They make me look like a sadistic monster who likes nothing better than to drown pussycats and tear wings off butterflies!

MRS. MARA: Quiet, dear. Tommy's still awake.

MARA: Oh. Oh, yeah.

MRS. MARA: It'd— it'd just break his heart if he knew what his daddy is doing.

MARA: I'm doing my job as assistant district attorney.

MRS. MARA: Well, I'm starting to agree with those reporters. Mr. Kringle looks like a very nice old man and I don't see why you have to keep persecuting him!

MARA: I'm not persecuting him, I'm prosecuting him! I like the old man, too, but there's nothing I can do about it.

MRS. MARA: You know something, Thomas? Sometimes I wish I'd married a butcher or... or a plumber!

MARA: Well, if I lose this case, it's very possible you'll get your wish! ...R. H. Macy. *(Fading)* I— I wonder what he's gonna pull tomorrow.

MUSIC #37: COURT BUMPER A

SCENE 7

NY COUNTY COURTHOUSE, NYC. DAY.

(JUDGE, FRED, MARA & MACY)

WALLA-WALLA: FADE IN BUZZ OF COURTROOM CROWD.

SOUND: BANG OF GAVEL

WALLA-WALLA: crowd quiets.

JUDGE: Proceed with the witness, Mr. Gailey.

FRED: Now then, Mr. Macy, if you recognize the defendant, please tell us who he is.

MACY: Why, Kris Kringle, of course.

FRED: Do you believe him to be of sound mind?

MACY: Sound mind? I wish I had a dozen like him.

FRED: Mr. Macy, you are under oath. Do you believe that man is Santa Claus?

MACY: Well, now that's, uh, rather a delicate, uh...

MUSIC #37A: IN MACY'S HEAD

(Muttering, to himself)

Think, just think of those headlines tomorrow, R.H.! "Macy Admits His Santa Claus is Fraud!" Think of all you'll lose. Think of all Gimbel will gain. Gimbel, Gimbel... curse you, Gimbel!

FRED: What's that, Mr. Macy?

MACY *(sputtering)*: Nothing, Mr. Gailey, nothing.

FRED: Mr. Macy, please answer my question. *(Pointed)* Is that man Santa Claus?

Long beat. Silence.

MACY *(firmly)*: Yes! In my opinion, he most certainly is!

WALLA-WALLA: courtroom reactions (big!).

One more thing, your Honor. I see my employee, Mr. Sawyer, sitting in this courtroom. May I address him?

JUDGE: Certainly.

MACY: Mr. Sawyer? Just for the record— you're fired! *(Moving off the stand, in glee)* Good-bye, Santa Claus!

KRIS: Good-bye, Mr. Macy! Thank you!

WALLA-WALLA: general hubbub.

MARA: Your Honor! There is no such person as Santa Claus, and everybody knows it!

FRED: Can you prove there isn't any?

MARA: I won't even try. I'll not waste the court's time with such childish nonsense. Your Honor, the prosecution requests an immediate ruling from this court. Is there or is there not a Santa Claus?

JUDGE: Well, now, uh— I, uh— The court will take a short recess to consider the question.

WALLA-WALLA: courtroom noise fades out.

MUSIC #37B: COURT BUMPER B

SCENE 8

JUDGE'S CHAMBERS (CONTINUOUS)

(JUDGE, CHARLEY)

ANNOUNCER: Judge Harper retreats to his chambers, only to find an old friend, a man of the cloth, waiting...

SOUND: DOOR CLOSES

CHARLEY: Hello, Henry.

JUDGE: Why, Charley! What are you doing here?

CHARLEY: Can't an old friend visit you in your chambers? And if you ask me, you never needed a friend like you do now. It's a good thing I'm a priest— you can confide in me.

JUDGE: This Kringle case? Oh, I certainly don't see what they're making such a fuss about.

CHARLEY: Henry, that's Santa Claus you've got out there. On trial for lunacy. This case is dynamite! And you're coming up for re-election soon.

JUDGE *(sadly)*: Charley, do you know what happened last night? Martha brought the grandchildren over. They— they wouldn't kiss Grandpa... They wouldn't even talk to me! *(Beat)* Little Billy kicked me in the shin.

CHARLEY: Ah, y'see what I mean? If you rule there is no Santa Claus, you'd better start looking for that chicken farm right now.

JUDGE: I'm a responsible judge! How can I seriously rule that there is a Santa Claus?

CHARLEY: Because of what happens if you don't! The kids read about it and they don't hang up their stockings. Now what happens to all the toys that are supposed to be in those stockings? Nobody buys them. The toy manufacturers have to lay off employees. By now, you've got the A.F. of L. and the C.I.O. against ya... Yes, and they're gonna say it with votes, see? Oh, and the department stores are gonna love you, too. *(Chuckling)* Yes sir, Henry. And what about the Salvation Army? They got a Santa Claus on every street corner. They take in a lot of money to help the poor! But go ahead, Henry. You go in there and rule there isn't any Santa Claus. But if you do, you can count on getting just two votes! Your own and that district attorney's out there.

JUDGE *(pause)*: One vote, Charley. He— he's a Republican... *(Moving off)* Oh, well, let's get this over with.

SOUND: DOOR CLOSES

MUSIC #37C: COURT BUMPER C

SCENE 9

COURTROOM (CONTINUOUS)

(JUDGE, MARA & FRED)

WALLA-WALLA: fade in buzz of courtroom crowd.

SOUND: BANG OF GAVEL

WALLA-WALLA: crowd quiets.

JUDGE: The, uh, the question of Santa Claus seems to be, uh, largely a matter of opinion. The, uh, tradition of American justice demands a broad and unprejudiced view of such a controversial matter.

MARA: But, your Honor!

JUDGE: This court, therefore, intends to keep its mind open. We shall ask for evidence on either side.

MARA: But the burden of proof clearly rests with my opponent. Can he produce any evidence to support his views?

FRED: If your Honor, please, I can. Will Thomas Mara please take the stand?

WALLA-WALLA: courtroom reacts.

MARA: Who, me?

FRED: No. Thomas Mara, Jr. I believe he and his mother are both in court today.

TOMMY *(super peppy)*: Hi, papa!

MARA *(in dismay)*: Hi...

FRED: Tommy, you know the difference between telling the truth and telling a lie, don't you?

TOMMY: Everybody knows you shouldn't tell a lie. Especially in court.

FRED: Do you believe in Santa Claus?

TOMMY: I sure do! Gosh, he gave me a brand new sled last year.

FRED: Now, uh, what does Santa Claus look like, Tommy?

TOMMY: Well, there he is sitting right over there.

WALLA-WALLA: Courtroom reactions.

MARA: Your Honor, I protest!

JUDGE: Overruled!

FRED: Tell me, Tommy, uh, why are you so sure there's a Santa Claus?

TOMMY: Because my papa told me so! Didn't you, Pop?!

Courtroom laughter!

FRED: And you believe your papa, don't you?

TOMMY: Sure I do. Papa wouldn't tell me anything that wasn't so, would you, papa?

FRED: Thank you, Tommy. You can go back to your mother now.

TOMMY: See you later, papa!

MARA *(under his breath)*: You certainly will... Your Honor–

TOMMY *(to Kris)*: Don't forget, Santa Claus, this year I want a football helmet!

KRIS: Don't worry, Tommy, you'll get it.

MARA: Mr. Kringle, if you don't mind–

KRIS: I'm sorry, sir.

MARA: Your Honor, the State of New York concedes the existence of a Santa Claus. But, in so conceding, we demand that Mr. Gailey stop representing and presenting personal opinion as evidence. I insist he submit authority to prove that Mr. Kringle here is the one and only Santa Claus.

JUDGE: Your point is well taken, Mr. Mara. Well, Mr. Gailey, are you prepared to show that Mr. Kringle is Santa Claus on the basis of unprejudiced authority?

FRED *(beat)*: Not just now, your Honor. I– I ask for an adjournment until this time tomorrow.

JUDGE: Thank heaven! *(Quickly)* Oh, I mean, very well. Court's adjourned till tomorrow afternoon.

SOUND: GAVEL BANGS

MUSIC #38: MARCH & TANNENBAUM

SCENE 10

DORIS' APARTMENT – THAT NIGHT
(DORIS & SUSAN)

ANNOUNCER: Normally, perusing the papers for good old fashioned news lightens the spirits of Doris and Susan. Tonight, together in their apartment, both search for hope in the dark...

DORIS: Now, come, Susan, dear, finish your supper.

SUSAN: But I can't, mother. All those things they're saying in the newspapers about Mr. Kringle and Mr. Gailey.

DORIS: They're having this trial because he says he's Santa Claus.

SUSAN: He's so— He's so kind and nice and jolly. He's not like anyone else I know. He must be Santa.

DORIS: You know something? I think perhaps you're right.

SUSAN: Is Mr. Kringle sad now, Mother?

DORIS: I'm afraid he must be.

SUSAN: Then I'll write him a letter. Maybe that'll make him feel better.

SONG #39: I BELIEVE IN YOU

(Singing)

DEAR MR. KRINGLE, I HOPE YOU'RE WELL
AND THAT YOU'RE NOT FEELING LOW
I'M NOT WRITING TO ASK FOR PRESENTS
I JUST WANTED YOU TO KNOW:

I BELIEVE IN GIANTS
FLOATING THROUGH THE STREETS OF THE CITY
I BELIEVE IN MICKEY MOUSE
I BELIEVE IN FELIX, THE KITTY

I BELIEVE IN PRETENDING
I BELIEVE IT'S THE ONE KEY
UNLOCKING THE WAY TO BE ANYTHING
EVEN A MONKEY

I CAN MAKE A SNOWBALL IN SUMMER
I CAN FLY WITH BIRDS IN THE AIR
I HAVE BEEN TO THE IMAGINE NATION
AND I LIKE IT THERE

SUSAN (CONT'D):

I CAN SEE THE WORLD IN A SNOWFLAKE
ALL BECAUSE OF YOU
AND THOUGH, I COULDN'T BEFORE
NOW, I BELIEVE IN YOU

DON'T FORGET WHO YOU ARE
OR WHAT YOU'VE DONE
DON'T FORGET ALL THE MIRACLES
YOU'VE BEGUN

DON'T FORGET WHAT YOU'RE PART OF
ALMOST SINCE THE START OF
ALWAYS THERE AT THE HEART OF
CHRISTMAS DAY

BUT THE ONE THING I DON'T HAVE TO DO
IS PRETEND FOR A MOMENT THAT I BELIEVE IN YOU
AND THAT'S BECAUSE I DO.

(Speaking)

All finished. Where shall I send it?

DORIS: Send it to the New York County Courthouse. Just a moment before you seal it– I'd like to write something.

SOUND: WRITING, THEN SEALING ENVELOPE

SUSAN: What did you write, Mother?

DORIS *(sings)*: "I BELIEVE IN YOU TOO. Doris." Go take your bath, darling.

SUSAN *(moving away)*: Yes mother.

DORIS *(to herself, chuckling)*: She addressed it to Santa Claus! That sweet, sweet...

MUSIC #40: IDEA & ZIPPING

(Beat, considering)

She addressed it... to Santa Claus... *(Calling out)* Susan, dear! I'll be right back. I'm heading down the hall to Mr. Gailey's!

SUSAN *(muted, in the bathroom)*: All right, Mother! But you can call him "Fred"– I know how you really feel about him!

SCENE 11

FRED'S APARTMENT (CONTINUOUS)

(DORIS & FRED)

ANNOUNCER: Zipping down the hall, Doris gives Fred's apartment door the what for!

SOUND: FEVERISH KNOCKING ON DOOR

DORIS: Fred! Oh, Fred, please open up!

FRED *(from inside)*: Just a moment, Doris.

SOUND: DOOR UNLOCKING, OPENING

Now what's–? Hey! I was going to invite you in, but you almost knocked me over!

DORIS: I'm sorry, Fred.

FRED: And I'm sorry. Listen, Doris. I've been thinking–

DORIS: I've been thinking too. That's why I'm here.

FRED: The way we last left things. It wasn't fair of me to–

DORIS: And it wasn't fair of me either. But you need to listen–

FRED: I know. And I have listened. To my heart as well as my head, and–

DORIS: Fred, this letter–

FRED: I've been thinking– we need to meet in the middle of common sense and faith. You see, I l(ove you)–

DORIS: Fred, please!

MUSIC #40A: REUNION UNDERSCORE

Of course we're going to meet in the middle and make this work, of course you love me, and of course I love you! But right now, I need you to look at this letter. It could very well save Mr. Kringle and your reputation!

FRED: It's made out to Santa Claus... how nice.

DORIS: How many letters to Santa Claus do you suppose the Post Office has?

FRED: Oh I don't know, darling, probably... probably thousands...

A BEAT.

Doris, I love you!

SONG #41: USPS MARCH

MEN:

IF YOU WANT TO SEND A LETTER
TO THE ONE YOU LOVE

MEN (CONT'D):

IF YOU WANT TO LET THEM KNOW
THAT THEY'RE THE ONE YOU'RE THINKING OF
IF YOU WANT YOUR PACKAGES
DELIVERED EAST OR WEST
SEND IT WITH THE VERY VERY BEST
THE UNITED STATES POSTAL SERVICE
U.S.P.S.!

SCENE 12

NY COUNTY COURTROOM, NYC – DAY

(JUDGE, MARA, FRED, KRIS & POSTMAN)

MARA: And since the defense has been unable to submit one shred of proof that Kris Kringle is the one and only Santa Claus, and since tonight is Christmas Eve, I ask, your Honor, that these commitment papers be signed without further delay.

FRED: I protest! I do have evidence. During Mr. Mara's oration, the bailiff handed my client the evidence I refer to.

JUDGE: What evidence?

KRIS: This letter, your Honor.

JUDGE: Oh, yes, Mr. Kringle?

KRIS *(a bubbling joy)*: It's from Susan Walker. She believes in me! Oh, this letter means more to me than anything in the world.

FRED: That letter, your Honor, was delivered by the United States Post Office– an official agency of the federal government. The Post Office department is one of the largest business concerns in the world. Last year did a gross volume of over one billion dollars and this year–

MARA: Your Honor, I'm sure we're all gratified that the Post Office is getting along so well... But what bearing has it on the sanity of this man?!

FRED: My point is that the Post Office department is a model of efficiency. Furthermore, the laws of this country make it a criminal offense to willfully misdirect mail or intentionally deliver it to the wrong party.

MARA *(rapidly, at the end of his patience)*: The State of New York is second to none in its admiration of the Post Office department. We're very happy to concede that the Post Office department is authoritative, prosperous, and efficient.

FRED: Uh, for the record, Mr. Mara?

MARA: For the record. Anything to get on with this case.

FRED: Thank you. Your Honor, that letter just received by Mr. Kringle is positive proof that a competent–

MARA: One letter is hardly positive proof!

FRED: I have further exhibits, your Honor, but I– I hesitate to produce them.

JUDGE: Come, come, Mr. Gailey, put them here on my desk.

FRED: But, your Honor–

JUDGE: I said, put them on my desk!

FRED *(calling out)*: All right, boys! Bring 'em in!

WALLA-WALLA: Courtroom reactions– surprise!

MARA *(stunned)*: Your– Your Honor! What– what is this?

FRED: Postal carriers— please empty those mail sacks on Judge Harper's desk!

SOUND: MAIL SACKS PILED ON JUDGE'S DESK... CONTINUES IN BG

JUDGE *(sputtering in surprise)*: Well, but, uh—

FRED: Bring them all in or be fined for contempt of court!

JUDGE: Now, now, just a second here!

POSTMAN: Ah, we'll do it, your Honor. Through rain, through sleet, through courtrooms— anything! We deliver!

MEN:

THROUGH RAIN OR SNOW OR SLEET
ANY CLIMATE THAT ABOUNDS
WE'LL BRAVE ANY WEATHER
FOR SWIFT COMPLETION OF OUR ROUND

JUDGE: Mr. Gailey!

FRED: Your Honor, every one of those letters in every one of those mail sacks is addressed to Santa Claus. The Post Office delivered them. Therefore, the Post Office department, and the United States Government, recognizes Kris Kringle to be the one and only Santa Claus.

SOUND: GASP; PILING OF MAIL SACKS STOPS

JUDGE: Since the United States of America declares this man to be Santa Claus, this court will not dispute it! Case dismissed!

Cheers and applause, continues in bg.

And, for heaven's sake, get this mail out of my courtroom!

KRIS: Merry Christmas, your Honor! Merry Christmas, Mr. Mara!

MEN:

SO WHEN YOU NEED TO BRIDGE THE DISTANCE
QUICKER THAN THE REST
SEND YOUR POST
WITH THE FOLKS YOU TRUST THE MOST
THE VERY BEST!
THE UNITED STATES POSTAL SERVICE
U.S.P.S.!

WALLA-WALLA: Courtroom slowly fades out.

SCENE 13

MACY'S TOY DEPARTMENT – LATE AFTERNOON

(KRIS & DORIS)

ANNOUNCER: As soon as Kris got out of court, he went straight to Macy's to see Doris.

SOUND: MUSIC BOX

KRIS *(fading in)*: So as soon as I got out of court, I came straight to Macy's to see you, Doris.

DORIS: Oh, Kris, I'm so glad you won!

KRIS *(exhales in relief)*: Yes, well, Fred told me I had you to thank as well!

DORIS: It was a team effort.

KRIS: I don't doubt it. Well, we're having a big Christmas party at the Brooks Home tomorrow morning. I'd like so much to see you and Susan there.

DORIS: We'll be there, Kris. Oh, Kris, couldn't you— couldn't you come home now and have dinner with us?

KRIS *(incredulous)*: Now? Tonight? Me? My goodness, Doris, it's— it's Christmas Eve.

MUSIC #42 TIDINGS OF COMFORT AND JOY

MEN:
O TIDINGS OF COMFORT AND JOY

WOMEN:
GOD REST YE MERRY GENTLEMEN

MEN:
O TIDINGS OF COMFORT AND JOY

WOMEN:
TIDINGS OF COMFORT AND JOY

MEN:
GOD REST YE MERRY GENTLEMEN

QUARTET:
TIDINGS OF COMFORT AND JOY
GOD REST YE MERRY

SCENE 14

BROOKS HOME FOR THE ELDERLY, LONG ISLAND – CHRISTMAS DAY

(**KRIS, ALFRED, DORIS, FRED, SUSAN, MACY & GIMBEL**)

WALLA-WALLA: Fade in buzz of PARTYGOERS... continues in bg.

KRIS: Alfred, Alfred, look! Look who came all the way out here to the home, just for our Christmas party!

ALFRED: Kris, it's— it's Mr. Macy!

KRIS: Mr. Gimbel, too! And they're about to sing!

The actor playing both men sings a traditional holiday tune, back and forth as both MACY and GIMBEL.

AT THE ENTRANCEWAY:

MUSIC #43: FAITH UNDERSCORE

ANNOUNCER: Meanwhile, over at the other end of the party...

DORIS: But, Susie darling, you got so many presents.

SUSAN *(tearful)*: Not the one I wanted. Not the one Mr. Kringle was gonna get for me!

DORIS: Well, what was it?

SUSAN: It doesn't matter. I knew I wouldn't get it. But I thought he'd at least tell me why.

KRIS *(off)*: Susie? *(Moving closer)* I'm sorry, Susie. I tried my best, but—

SUSAN: You couldn't get it because you're not Santa Claus.

DORIS: Susan!

SUSAN: Just a nice old man, like mother said.

DORIS: But I was wrong when I told you that. You must believe in Mr. Kringle, and keep right on doing it. You must have faith in him.

SUSAN: But that's not practical— that doesn't make sense, mother!

DORIS: Faith is believing in things when common sense tells you not to.

SUSAN: What?!

DORIS: I mean, just because things don't turn out the way you want them to the first time, you've still got to believe in people. I found that out—

FRED: Hello, Doris.

DORIS: Fred!

SUSAN *(happily)*: Mr. Gailey! Mr. Gailey!

FRED: Merry Christmas, Susie!

SUSAN: Gosh, you just get here and we're ready to leave.

FRED: Oh, I've been here.

SUSAN: Oh.

FRED: And if you're ready to leave, I'll drive you home.

KRIS: Before you go— Here.

SOUND: RUSTLE OF PAPER

Here's a map I've made for you. You'll miss a lot of traffic. About four miles south, you will see Ashley Avenue. Now that's the street you want. Ashley Avenue.

FRED: Thanks, Kris. And Merry Christmas.

KRIS: Merry Christmas to you, Fred. And to you, my dear. And to you, Susan.

SONG #44: HARK! THE HERALD ANGELS SING

SUSAN: I believe, Mr. Kringle. I do. It's silly, I suppose. But I do.

KRIS: I know you do, my dear. And I believe in you.

MUSIC: up full for a moment, then crossfades with:

SOUND: CAR ENGINE, FOR A MOMENT, THEN IN BG

SCENE 15

INT. CAR/EXT. ASHLEY AVENUE – EARLY EVENING.

(DORIS, FRED & SUSAN)

DORIS: I don't understand it, Fred. The map Kris gave definitely says Ashley Avenue. We've been on Ashley Avenue now for–

SUSAN: Stop the car, Fred! Oh, stop the car, please!

DORIS: Susie, what is it, darling? What's the matter?

SOUND: CAR ENGINE SLOWS TO A STOP

SUSAN *(excited)*: There it is! The house! The house!

SOUND: CAR DOOR OPENS

FRED *(calls out)*: Susie!

SOUND: FAST SNOW FEET

DORIS: What in the world?

SOUND: FRONT DOOR OPENS

FRED: She's running into that house.

SOUND: TWO MORE CAR DOORS OPEN

DORIS: Well, at least there's no one home. It's brand new, it's just been built.

SOUND: TWO SETS OF SLOWER FEET THROUGH SNOW

FRED: Yeah. "For sale," it says. *(Reflective)* For sale...

DORIS *(fading out as she walks away)*: What on earth is that child up to?

SOUND: FEET STOP, DOOR OPENS

FRED *(fades in, calls)*: Susie! Hey, Susie!

SUSAN *(off)*: Here I am! Upstairs!

DORIS *(calling)*: Now, come right down! You know you shouldn't run around in other people's houses! *(Pause, quietly to Fred)* That's strange.

FRED: I'll say.

DORIS: No, no, I mean this house. I've seen this house somewhere, I know I have. Maybe in a magazine or–

SOUND: CHILD FEET RUNNING DOWNSTAIRS

SUSAN *(running in)*: Mother! It's our house! It's the one I asked him for– Mr. Kringle.

SOUND: FEET RUNNING OUT

DORIS: Mr. Kringle?

SUSAN: I know it is! Oh, you were right, Mommy, you were right!

FRED: Susie?

SUSAN: Mommy told me that if things didn't turn out just the way you wanted them at first, you've still gotta believe. And I kept believing! And you were right, Mommy. *(Moving off)* Mr. Kringle is Santa Claus!

SOUND: MORE CHILD FEET RUNNING

DORIS: Now where are you going?

SUSAN *(off)*: In back, to see if there's a swing!

SOUND: DOOR OPENS

(Fading out)

There is one, oh, there is one!

FRED: You told her that? About believing?

DORIS: Well– You told me, Fred.

FRED *(chuckles)*: The sign outside– "for sale," huh? Well, we can't let her down, can we?

DORIS: Oh, darling. I never really doubted you. It was just my silly common sense.

FRED: There's nothing silly about your common sense. *(Laughs)* Even makes sense to believe in us, now. Your brilliant idea about the mail, and my equally brilliant execution... we're a great team to take a little old man and legally prove to the world that he's Santa Claus. Now, you know that couldn't possibly be–

DORIS *(whispering)*: Fred!

FRED: What's the matter?

MUSIC #44A: THE CANE RETURNS

DORIS *(slowly, in awe)*: There. In the corner. By the fireplace.

FRED *(in wonder and disbelief)*: Oh, no. No.

DORIS: It– it can't be. It– it couldn't–

FRED: A cane. Kris' cane. There couldn't be two canes like this anywhere in the world. Carved out of an old sleigh.

DORIS: Silver handle and all.

FRED: Hey, you know something? Maybe we didn't do such a remarkable thing after all.

DORIS: Maybe it wasn't us at all...

SONG #45: MIRACLES

FRED:

MAYBE THERE IS SOMETHING
BIGGER THAN WE KNOW
SOMETHING AT THIS TIME OF YEAR
BEYOND THE FALLING SNOW

BEYOND THE DANCING LIGHTS
AND TINSEL ON THE TREE
THAT MAKES US INTO THE PEOPLE
WE ALWAYS WISH THAT WE COULD BE

MAYBE THERE ARE MIRACLES
WE CAN'T BEGIN TO UNDERSTAND

DORIS:

MAYBE THERE ARE MIRACLES
IF YOU JUST REACH OUT YOUR HAND

FRED:

IN A SEASON OF FORGIVING
WHERE WE ALL CAN START AGAIN
DO A BETTER JOB OF LIVING
GIVE KINDNESS TO YOUR FELLOW MEN

DORIS:

AND IF YOU BELIEVE IN THEM
AND THEY BELIEVE IN YOU
IT CAN MAKE A MIRACLE
HAPPEN TO YOU

FRED:

SO, PEACE ON EARTH, GOODWILL TO MEN
BELIEVE YOU CAN BEGIN AGAIN
JUST LIKE IN A CHRISTMAS SONG
BUT CHRISTMAS IS A STATE OF MIND
HAVE FAITH IN SOMEONE AND YOU'LL FIND
MAYBE THERE ARE MIRACLES
MIRACLES THE WHOLE YEAR LONG

ANNOUNCER: Their faith restored, Doris, Susan, Fred, the citizens of New York, and the citizens of the globe, perhaps, have found a reason to believe not only in an idea but in a tangible, flesh and blood connection to one another. They're filled with that intangible dreamstuff— hope. They'll take care of each other, now. They'll love their fellows and they'll soar through the snow. *(After a beat)* Will you?

ALL:

SO, PEACE ON EARTH, GOODWILL TO MEN
BELIEVE YOU CAN BEGIN AGAIN
JUST LIKE IN A CHRISTMAS SONG
BUT CHRISTMAS IS A STATE OF MIND
HAVE FAITH IN SOMEONE AND YOU'LL FIND
THAT MAYBE THERE ARE MIRACLES
MIRACLES THE WHOLE YEAR LONG

ANNOUNCER: Thank you, ladies and gentlemen. And now, help me in recognizing the talents of our stars!

CURTAIN CALL:

Wallace Ainsley! Olivia Glatt! Grady Williams! Cordelia Ragsdale! Gracie DeMarco! Kristofer van Lisberg! And I'm Alex Mialdo for KSDMT!

MUSIC: a final flourish, to:

SONG #46: CAROL-PALOOZA

MEN:

O COME ALL YE FAITHFUL

QUARTET:

SILENT NIGHT, HOLY NIGHT
ALL IS CALM, AND

MEN:

EVERYTHING IS LOOKING BRIGHT!

QUARTET:

HARK THE HERALD ANGEL SING,
HERE WE COME A-CAROLING

STAR OF WONDER, STAR OF NIGHT,
STAR WITH ROYAL BEAUTY BRIGHT
WESTWARD LEADING, STILL PROCEEDING
GUIDE US TO THY PERFECT LIGHT

LOVE AND JOY COME TO YOU,
HAVE A MERRY CHRISTMAS, TOO
AND GOD BLESS YOU AND SEND YOU A HAPPY NEW YEAR
YES, WE WISH YOU A HAPPY EVERY YEAR!
HAPPY HOLIDAYS!
HAPPY ALL THE DAYS!

ALL: Merry Christmas, everyone!

END

ABOUT STAGE RIGHTS

Made in the USA
Monee, IL
05 September 2022

13216037R00049